Praise for Robert David

"Few have thought as d
questions as a super-sma
officer named Robert D

> —Alvin and Heidi Toffler, authors of *War & Anti-War:*
> *Survival at the Dawn of the 21st Century*

"Robert Steele is unusual for an American . . . he is clearly internationalist in his orientation. He has written a book that can bring us together in facing our greatest enemies: ignorance, poverty, and mistrust."

> —Rear Admiral Hamit Gulemre Aybars,
> Turkish Navy (Retired)

"Robert Steele's vision for the future of intelligence is clearly 'internationalist' in nature. It focuses on regional partnerships . . . and on the value of open-source intelligence collection."

> —Rear Admiral Dr. Sigurd Hess, DE N(Ret.), Former
> Chief of Staff, Allied Command Baltic Approaches

"Constantly committed to truth and honesty, [his work] demonstrates his ability to grasp the real issues and to take into account the views and concerns of men of good will from all nations and all cultures."

> —Admiral Pierre Lacoste, French Navy (Ret.),
> Former Director of Foreign Intelligence

"Robert Steele goes well beyond the original visions of the best of the Directors of Central Intelligence, and has crafted a brilliant, sensible, and honorable future for the intelligence profession."

— Major General Oleg Kalugin, KGB (Ret.),
Former Elected Deputy to the Russian Parliament

"Over a broad canvas reflecting the changing nature of information and information technologies, Robert Steele lays the foundation for the future of e-intelligence."

— Commodore Patrick Tyrrell, OBE,
Royal Navy, United Kingdom

"Steele consistently has been well ahead of the pack in his appreciation for everything from open-source research to the implications of technology... his work thrills with its insights and ideas."

— Ralph Peters, author of *Fighting for the Future:
Will America Triumph?*

"Steele's concept is simple: Empower the citizen and private sector to gather and analyze intelligence so that we can make informed decisions [using] Open-Source Intelligence gathering [that] is faster, smarter, cheaper...."

— Robert Young Pelton, author of *World's Most Dangerous
Places* and producer of *Come Back Alive*

"Robert Steele deserves our admiration and our focused attention for bringing the idea of open-source information to the fore. His passion to serve the nation by developing this new approach... is exemplary."

— Lieutenant General Patrick Hughes, U.S. Army (Ret.),
Former Director, Defense Intelligence Agency

The Open-Source Everything Manifesto

Transparency, Truth, and Trust

Robert David Steele

Foreword by Howard Bloom

Berkeley, California

Published by Evolver Editions, an imprint of North Atlantic Books
P.O. Box 12327
Berkeley, California 94712

Cover art direction and design by michaelrobinsonnyc.com
Book design by Brad Greene
Printed in the United States of America

The Open-Source Everything Manifesto: Transparency, Truth, and Trust is sponsored by the Society for the Study of Native Arts and Sciences, a nonprofit educational corporation whose goals are to develop an educational and cross-cultural perspective linking various scientific, social, and artistic fields; to nurture a holistic view of arts, sciences, humanities, and healing; and to publish and distribute literature on the relationship of mind, body, and nature.

North Atlantic Books' publications are available through most bookstores. For further information, visit our website at www.northatlanticbooks.com or call 800-733-3000.

Library of Congress Cataloging-in-Publication Data

Steele, Robert David, 1952–
    The open-source everything manifesto : transparency, truth, and trust / Robert David Steele ; foreword by Howard Bloom.
       p. cm.
    Summary: "Written by a former CIA covert ops and intelligence expert, The Open-Source Everything Manifesto provides a roadmap for empowering the public to return to an informed, engaged democracy of, by, and for the people"—Provided by publisher.
    ISBN 978-1-58394-443-1
    1. Open source intelligence—United States. I. Title.
JK468.I6S744 2012
327.12–dc23
                                                              2012005230

2 3 4 5 6 7 8 UNITED 18 17 16 15 14
Printed on recycled paper

CONTENTS

Put enough eyeballs on it, no bug is invisible.

~

The truth at any cost lowers all other costs.

FOREWORD

I've known Robert D. Steele for over fifteen years now, ever since he invited me to speak in 1996 to a gathering of international spies, intelligence managers, and professional intelligence analysts in Washington, DC.

Then in 2005, what looked like peaceful revolution showed up in the streets of Egypt and Lebanon. But it was hard to tell whether the footage of protests blossoming on Middle Eastern TV stations showed the activity of a lunatic fringe or revealed something that went far deeper. So at three AM one night, I convened an online group that included: a member of the State Department; one of UNESCO's top hundred intellectuals of the Islamic world; the former editor-in-chief of *Newsweek;* a tiny handful of others ... and Robert D. Steele. Steele said it was one of the best brain trusts since Winston Churchill's late-night brainstorming sessions and FDR's kitchen cabinet. But he was prejudiced. He was part of the group. (Our Islamic intellectual, Dr. Munawar Anees, by the way, made a powerful case that the Arab lust for democracy was real.)

In all these encounters, I had the same reaction that Howard Rheingold and John Perry Barlow had when they spoke at Steele's first conference in 1992: Robert D. Steele was onto something.

What was it? Let's start with Julian Assange[1] and Wiki-Leaks.[2] In 2010, when WikiLeaks' materials blasted their way into the headlines, I loathed Assange for his dislike of the United States. And I felt I was also supposed to be outraged by the carefully spooned-out flow of Assange's WikiLeaks. Outrage was my duty as a patriotic American. But I wasn't angered. My real feelings were held down below, way down at a non-verbal level. Why? Because I had been aware of many of the truths in WikiLeaks' revelations. I had shared many of the same opinions of the world leaders we are forced to deal with. The only truly objectionable material in Assange's leaks was the names of sources, names whose publication could get those sources killed and could shut down future flows of vital information.

I don't know about you, but I felt cheated by the fact that the government would not share its thinking with me. Maybe you are asking: Why in the world should our government share its thought process with the likes of you and me? You and I are just water molecules in a vast sea, grains of sand on an enormous beach. Surely we don't have the level of sophistication it takes to understand the subtle currents of international affairs. But research on collective smarts among every sort of beast from bacteria and baboons to Marxists, capitalists, and kleptocrats indicates one thing. A whompingly impressive processing power emerges when when we are all used together as components in a learning machine. What's more, my books—books like *The Lucifer Principle* and *Global Brain*—use biological paradoxes like depression and programmed cell death to make the case that our insecurities and our blue moods evolved to make us exactly that—modules.

Macroprocessors in a parallel distributed supercomputer. Neurons in a collective brain. Participants in a group IQ.

But secrecy has prevented people like George W. Bush, Condoleezza Rice, Hilary Clinton, and Barack Obama from using this slumbering group IQ. The result? Our "intelligence" gave us the clues to 9/11 in advance. But it failed to connect the dots. It failed to see the big picture. And our "intelligence" told us there were weapons of mass destruction in Iraq when, in fact, there were not.

Faulty intelligence—dumbed-down intelligence— pushed us into a nine-year war, the Iraq War. A war that cost us more than a trillion dollars[3] and gave us the biggest deficit in world history. What dumbs down our intelligence? Steele argues that it is the top-secret nature of our national "intelligence" programs.

There is a name for the alternative, a name for the kind of collective intelligence that Robert David Steele has been advocating and that Julian Assange was practicing. Steele calls it "Open-Source Intelligence." And you're about to read what it is. What's more, you're about to read how Steele, an intelligence professional who has been both a spy under deep cover and a co-creator of the Marine Corps Intelligence Center, came to realize that open-source intelligence is a necessity. This realization went hand in hand with his observation of something else crucial—that intelligence done in top-secrecy mode does not work!

Robert D. Steele argues more coherently than anyone I know what an open-source intelligence is and how it can operate. He reveals how he tried to work from the inside to bring open-source intelligence to the military and to something even more vital: to our policy-makers. In fact, Steele saw firsthand how open-source intelligence can run rings around normal top-secret intelligence. And he saw from the inside exactly why.

He saw why our so-called intelligence has been so retarded that it has endangered our economy and cast a pall over our future. He saw why the intelligence that is supposed to lead us to victory is consistently defeating us.

What did Robert David Steele see? The answers are in *The Open-Source Everything Manifesto: Transparency, Truth, and Trust.*

— Howard Bloom
February 3, 2012

> Government is not built to perceive great truths; only people can perceive great truths. Governments specialize in small and intermediate truths. They have to be instructed by their people in great truths. And the particular truth in which they need instructions today is that new means for meeting the largest problems on earth have to be created.
>
> —Norman Cousins[1]

I realized in 1988 that my life as a spy specializing in secrets was not only unproductive, it was in sharp opposition to what we actually need: full access to true information, to the complete diversity of views on any given issue, and consequently, the ability to create Open-Source Intelligence (OSINT). OSINT provides the foundation for direct democracy: participatory intelligence (decision-support), open-source policy-making, and participatory budgeting.

I bring to the writing of this manifesto my decades of professional experience in the field of intelligence-gathering, as well as a deep desire to help nurture a global movement to share information and knowledge as widely as possible. The new meme is a bit convoluted but it captures the universality of all minds, all information, all languages, all the time: Multinational, Multiagency, Multidisciplinary, Multidomain Information- Sharing and Sense-Making (M4IS2).[2]

Alvin Toffler anticipated this day in his book *PowerShift: Knowledge, Wealth, and Violence at the Edge of the 21st Century*,[3] where he developed the idea of information/intelligence as a substitute for wealth, violence, labor, time, and space. Open-Source Everything—and in the information arena, M4IS2—is, I believe, the foundation of a prosperous world at peace. A public able to access all information all the time, and the obliteration of secrecy and top-down decision-making, will be among the hallmarks of a new era in our civilization. Both of these require integrity as core attribute.[4]

As a professional intelligence officer who held Top Secret and Sensitive Compartmented Information (TS/SCI) clearances for thirty years (1976–2006), I was originally focused on national security secrets and employed by the U.S. government. With time and experience I slowly realized that the vast troves of "open" sources of information—meaning what is accessible to anyone willing to look or listen—are more reliable and more useful than "secret" sources that have built-in obstacles to validation and accountability.

Matt Drudge and the *Drudge Report* are a classic example of the changing dynamics of how the public is informed. He broke the Monica Lewinsky story at a time when the corporate media was holding back because of its incestuous relationship with the two-party tyranny that strives to control what We the People can learn.

Since then a vibrant literature has emerged about Collective Intelligence, with titles using that term and similar ones such as *Army of Davids*, *Wisdom of the Crowds*, *Smart Mobs*, *Here Comes Everybody*, and *Groundswell.*[5]

What all this boils down to is that normal average human beings, when they share information openly with one another and engage in respectful deliberative dialog, always, without exception, arrive at better conclusions than experts or elites who rely on "secret" information and generally have hidden agendas enabled by secrecy combined with public ignorance and apathy.

I am not alone in the conviction that real, lasting national security can best be obtained through complete transparency of government, business, and other facets of society, and this includes open access to all of the many available types of information. This is intelligence with integrity, in the public interest—the alternative to hierarchical, elitist organizations that allow the few to profit at the expense of the many. Of course, citizens must be educated, involved, and have the interest in civic and other affairs to maximize the use of public intelligence. The establishment of a transparent and open government, open society, and open economy that is truly of, by, and for We the People *requires* the self-actualization of We the People.

What we have learned in the past half century—and in the past decade most painfully—is that top-down governance has become corrupt and does not work. Central planning does not work—the nanny state attempts to micro-manage what it does not understand, glossing over high crimes by financial enterprises that have bought Congressional blindness. Attempts to conceal the truth from the public that have worked in the past no longer work, and this is what has created the "cognitive dissonance" that is at the root of all revolutions. That is what has made Occupy Wall Street the potent force that it is, a force with more tools at its disposal than existed in Eastern Europe, sufficient at the time to depose the Soviet empire. One could argue that the American Empire has already been deposed; only in Washington, DC, and on Wall Street are they either in complete denial or making preparations for the last loot-fest before abandoning the ship of state they have sunk with greed. On the bright side, we have the promise of today's rising digital youth.

> The youth of humanity all around our planet are intuitively revolting from all sovereignties and political ideologies. The youth of Earth are moving intuitively toward an utterly classless, raceless, omnicooperative, omniworld humanity.
> —R. Buckminster Fuller[6]

What *does* work is agility at the lowest point in the system, and spontaneous agility across the system by a "mesh" of autonomous individuals who can Observe, Orient, Decide, and Act (OODA),[7] all without central direction or permission.

The U.S. government does not study anything holistically. Everything is studied and justified in isolation from all else. We, as a collective, can do much better. The future of intelligence is not secret, not federal, and not expensive. It is about transparency, truth, and trust.

Here's the bottom line: The secret world of intelligence—at least in the United States of America—represents everything that is wrong with the government, the industrial era, our financial-economic system, and our ethics. It was in 1988 that I first realized, beyond a shadow of a doubt, that the U.S. government is "the emperor wearing no clothes," ignorant of most of what goes on in the world, substituting ideology for intelligence, and expensive, largely useless contracting and technology for thinking. We lack intelligence as well as integrity in that we are spending $80 billion[8] a year on secret collection sources and methods, processing virtually none of that, and producing, in the words of General Tony Zinni, USMC (Retired), "at best" four percent of what the President or a major commander needs to know, and nothing for everyone else.[9]

The government is not reporting or even perceiving the truths—the true costs, the true options—that need to be perceived in the public interest. Hence, we need a new craft of intelligence that focuses on creating public intelligence in the public interest.[10] Instead of a top-heavy, opaque, centralized, and rigidified system that misses the big picture and rewards a few at the expense of the many, it is possible to create—at a fraction of the cost of what we spend now on largely worthless secret sources and methods—a "Smart Nation"[11] in which a mature decision-support function educates and enables every citizen to be a collector, producer, and consumer of legal, ethical, open-source intelligence, and also to be a vibrant member of the authentic intelligence community of the whole—humanity connected as one, thinking as one, acting as one. Every citizen must be actively aware of, participating in, and overseeing research,[12] and that research should be focused on creating prosperity and peace, not war and poverty or suicidal seeds.[13]

Transparency, which engenders truth, is the foundation for all this.

This book is intended to be a catalyst for citizen dialog and deliberation, and for inspiring the continued evolution of a nation in which all citizens realize our shared aspiration of direct democracy—direct informed democracy.

Nothing would please me more, nor allow me to contribute to the future of humanity more ably, than to see these recommendations for creating public intelligence adopted and acted upon in the public interest, thus enabling informed participatory democracy. We the People must *choose* to be active.

As Occupy struggles to invent (or re-invent) a form of community decision-making that is open, accountable, and effective, their greatest challenge appears to lie with two of these three features: accountable and effective. This manifesto is a "call to arms," not only for Occupy,[14] which can be considered the soul of the working class re-emergent, but for all of us—Independents, members of the political parties shut out of the existing electoral process by the two-party tyranny,[15] and the moderate members of the two parties captured by extremists and ideological politicians that monopolize the privilege of looting the public treasury, moderates who no longer consider their work or their political party structure—Republican or Democratic—to be of, by, or for We the People in any sense of the word.

Open-Source Everything is our path to power, peace, and prosperity, a restoration of the sensibility of the indigenous peoples of the world whose sacred knowledge we in the "advanced" West have disdained at our own peril.[16] Open-Source Everything reconnects us all to the root power of the cosmic universe, restores our harmony, and unleashes our inherent gifts of innovation, entrepreneurship, and generosity. I hope this book can be a harbinger of a new paradigm, pointing to a direction that we can go with relative ease (away from war and domestic corruption) to achieve our goal of a world that works for all.

Homo sapiens is the "Wild Card." Being is a mystery, Nature is a given, Science is a process, and Community—a prosperous world at peace—is a goal. The human species is the 900-pound gorilla that has the capacity to self-destruct for lack of temperance, or to become One with God through transparency, truth, and trust.[17]

— Robert David Steele
　 Oakton, Virginia
　 February 5, 2012

CHAPTER 1

Open Sesame

Open-Source Everything is a cultural and philosophical concept that is essential to creating a prosperous world at peace, a world that works for one hundred percent of humanity. As we know, the industrial-era formations of state and company and religion do not meet all our needs—they are exclusive rather than inclusive, hierarchical rather than egalitarian. They also encourage corruption and allow an egregious concentration of wealth in the hands of a few. Completely apart from the ethical atrocity, any concentration of this nature throws entire economies

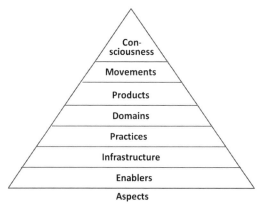

Figure 1: The Open-Source Pyramid

out of balance. They become dysfunctional, and the "seed corn" of an economy, We the People, the "ninety-nine percent," find ourselves being eaten by what is in essence a moral fungus or cancer spawned by the "one percent."

The universe of Open-Source Everything can be visualized as a pyramid that ranges from concepts through practices and products to movements and consciousness. It is, in other words, potentially pervasive.[1]

Open Source is both a concept and a method. Adopting an open-source approach to everything at the local, state, and national levels might look like this below.

Using Figure 2 as an outline, we can see how life would be affected by an Open-Source Everything approach, with the deliberate and direct outcome of RESILIENCE.

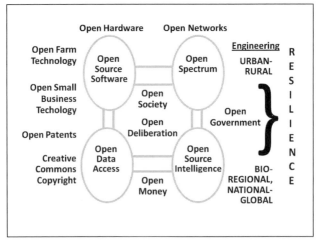

Figure 2: Basic Open-Source Approach to Resilience

The core concept here, one that Buckminster Fuller would endorse, is of achieving ZERO RESISTANCE in the transfer of energy and information. Put in other terms (that Occupy, among other movements, would appreciate), the objective is to eradicate CORRUPTION and all "burdens" on human activity that have been contrived and imposed without the consent of the governed. Corruption and lies are "resistance" to optimal functionality. They are also not patriotic and are often impeachable acts in the public sector, tantamount to organized criminal activity in the private sector.[2]

In an open-source community, all costs are minimized and benefits are optimized. The combination of Open-Source Hardware, Free/Open-Source Software (F/OSS), Open Data Access (ODA), Open-Source Intelligence (OSINT), and Open Spectrum (unconstrained access to all frequencies, none sold or assigned to specific organizations or functions) makes information-sharing—including education, intelligence or decision-support, and research—virtually free... and not merely free, but a catalyst for the creation of infinite wealth for all those "jacked in" to the World Brain, including the five billion poor, if we do the right thing.

The widespread adoption of copyright and Open Patents[3] allows communities to rapidly build for themselves fully functioning engines, vehicles, power tools, and all other needed equipment, using readily available components, while avoiding esoteric materials including rare earths. This concept redirects "commerce" from the goal of profit for the few to the goal of utility for the many at the lowest possible cost.

On this foundation, Open Deliberation and Open Money support Open Government and Open Society. Transparency and truth are the predominant attributes of the Open-Source Everything ecology, and trust is the tangible, persistent, and most valuable "spiritual energy" that sustains the community, ensuring resilience and sustainability. Trust between people is a substitute for money created by predatory organizations such as banks, which counterfeit "credit" they do not have to earn profits they do not merit.[4]

It is my thesis that the "Open" meme, first proven with Free/Open-Source Software, is now ready to be applied to the creation of Open Government and Open Society, with one big change from prevailing and preliminary practices: we create what we need in the way of Open-Source Everything, rather than being satisfied with lip service (Open Government) or foundation tokenism (Open Society). Creating an Open-Source Everything community on Earth will demand strength of will and stringent ethics. It will be done in the face of fierce opposition from industrial-era governments and corporations too long accustomed to hiding behind secrecy and externalizing costs (for example, selling bottled water or gasoline at a low price that does not factor in the costs to the public of waste, pollution, and depletion of scare resources). It will probably succeed one transitional local community at a time,[5] *but* I believe that this period in and around the year 2012 is a time of potential transformation in which organized people can beat organized money without violence.

It is vital that Open not be confused with Free. Our model is the Free/Open-Source Software community, where open means open to inspection, all code visible and accounted for. It does not mean that the software is of necessity free—some will be, some will not be. The Red Hat community is a model for how to mix volunteer, free orchestrated, and for-fee commercial services, centered on the openness of the code, the transparency of what each individual and organization is seeking to accomplish, and the common utility that each participant derives, not necessarily equally, but each according to their contribution and need.

Free/Open-Source Software is both safer and vastly cheaper than proprietary software. The proponents of this movement are the model for a global Open-Source Intelligence network that leverages a mix of Open Data Access and a vast number of human beings who are able to operate in all languages, all the time. This network is capable of doing what no other network—and certainly no government or corporation—can aspire to: tell the truth, the whole truth, all of the time, rooted in transparency and building trust—this is the alchemy of the twenty-first century: share information, earn trust. Transparency, not secrecy, is what produces validated intelligence (decision-support) that is truthful and trustworthy and therefore priceless.

The global implication of F/OSS and OSINT, when

combined with a long overdue global migration to Open Spectrum, is quite straightforward: the three together with Open Hardware make possible the Autonomous Internet[6] and the emergence of the World Brain and Global Game.[7]

The World Brain is the 24/7 connection of all human minds in all languages to one another and to all information in all languages and mediums.

The Global Game can be described as the melding of the World Brain with the "Six Bubbles" concept devised by the twenty-four co-founders of the Earth Intelligence Network, a 501(c)3 committed to creating public intelligence in the public interest. These are illustrated in Figure 3.

Various thinkers on these topics helped me make the connection between free, infinitely scalable information technology—also known as liberation technology—and creating a prosperous world at peace.[8]

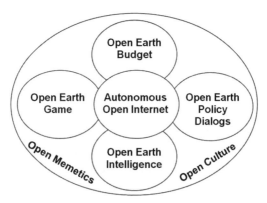

**Figure 3: "Six Bubbles" Approach to
Open-Source Everything**

Liberation technology is distinct from open-source technology primarily because the function of liberation can be achieved with proprietary and expensive technology, which are not open-source. One example is the leasing of satellites to provide for direct links from ground stations in repressive countries—ground stations that are not easy to detect because they are sending and receiving "straight up." Another is the purchase of encryption technologies including those that are "invisible" to censors, vanishing into photographs, a form of encryption known as steganography (hidden messages, often encrypted, inside of photographs). Where open-source technology excels is in scaling up—there is no way the five billion poor are going to be connected, much less educated, without a massive adoption of open-source technology such as has occurred recently within the universities of India.[9]

Liberation technology creates wealth, and open-source technology creates wealth. In both instances the "center of gravity" for dramatic change toward resilience and sustainability is the human brain mass of the five billion poor—the one billion rich have failed to "scale." The human brain is the one unlimited resource we have on Earth.[10] The potential for innovation and entrepreneurship on the part of the five billion poor is the most under-developed and under-utilized resource. For lack of simple inexpensive hand-held devices and access via those devices to more sophisticated call centers that can educate them "one cell call at a time" (as envisioned by the Earth Intelligence

Network), the five billion poor live in desperate poverty and grinding subsistence mode.[11]

I leave the details of intellectual property and copyright to others, but I subscribe to the Creative Commons concepts of Lawrence Lessig.[12]

Open-Source Everything scales that philosophy to encompass all human activity, all creations by humans, and human access to all historical knowledge.

The future must be open, it must empower all human minds all the time, and it must respect the reality that the future will be defined by the poor, not by the rich. What this means is not that the poor will be with us forever and that we must define our world to their condition, but rather that the mathematics is simple: one billion rich adhering to industrial-era concepts of secrecy, selfishness, and hierarchy cannot elevate the five billion poor; only the five billion poor can do that. If one adds the concept of compound interest, then it follows that the waste of the one billion rich can only be contained, neutralized, and ultimately displaced by the right living of the five billion poor whose aggregate minds can move in a righteous direction—toward creating a prosperous world at peace.

What we can do is focus on empowering the five billion poor with access to the Internet and free to very low cost cellular capabilities such that they apply their five billion minds, their five billion bundles of energy and entrepreneurship, to create infinite wealth for themselves. TIRED: Give them fish. TIRED: Teach them to fish. WIRED: Give them information tools and access to information to create infinite substitutes for fishing and fish.[13]

What has been lacking to date in the open world has been a strategic analytic model that allows shared information to leave no fraud, waste, or abuse (corruption) unnoticed, and to harmonize a diversity of endeavors without imposing "control."

Although I have written multiple books on the "how" of information sharing,[14] it was not until I was inspired by the Collective Intelligence movement and came face to face with the Web 2.0 thinking of so many emergent pathfinders that I realized the value of my two decades of work as a contribution to the Open-Source Everything era that begins in 2012.[15]

We are all in the process of "changing the game."

Changing the Game

Tom Atlee, co-founder of the Co-Intelligence Institute and author of *The Tao of Democracy: Using Co-Intelligence to Create a World that Works for All*,[16] as well as the more recent *Reflections on Evolutionary Activism: Essays, Poems and Prayers from an Emerging Field of Sacred Social Change*,[17] has been the most important influence on my thinking and feeling since I first discovered his work. I got to know him after he spoke at one of my annual conferences for mid-career intelligence professionals.

Below I illustrate the contrast between what I'll call "Epoch A," the millennium of human organization characterized by increasing hierarchy, hoarding, and "command and control" from above, with "Epoch B," the millennium of restored human community character-ized (as were our indigenous forebears) by a flattening of decision-making with processes that are multicultural, deeply appreciative of diversity, replete with integrity, and very much "bottom up," harnessing the distributed intelligence of all.[18]

Figure 4 illustrates both the traditional form of organi-zation, called here "Epoch-A Leadership," and the emer-gent form, "Epoch-B Leadership." There are several major differences between the two: the first is that in relying on secret sources and methods that are not accountable to

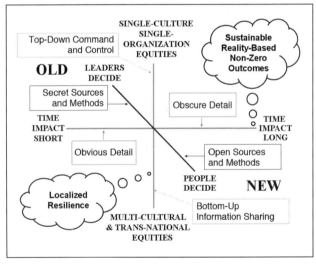

Figure 4: From Epoch A to Epoch B

the public and that are easy to manipulate in the absence of "sunshine" (Epoch A), the leadership becomes isolated from reality and swims in its own hubris, earnestly believing that it knows better than all others (or worse, could care less but is not held accountable for making decisions so obviously against the known facts).[19] From the inception of the industrial era, governments as well as corporations have been set up according to the Weberian concept of organizational design, one that emphasizes command and control over a rigidly structured "top-down" form.[20] The worst aspect of this form of organization has been its proclivity toward limiting and hoarding information, and abusing secrecy.[21]

This form of organization and its inherent practices in turn make possible predatory capitalism, virtual colonialism, and many other acts of greed and insensitivity.[22] Corruption is endemic[23] in Epoch-A hierarchies of government, banking, and business as well as in civil society (labor unions, religions) and in non-governmental organizations. Bureaucratic agencies and ambitious or misguided individuals hoard information for selfish ends rather than sharing information for the "good of the group," and in doing so, they sacrifice accountability and enable crime and treason. Government intelligence-gathering is conventionally focused on nuclear proliferation, terrorism, and transnational crime; in the emerging new epoch we are focused on preventing genocide and other atrocities, as well as on creating the necessary infrastructure for global networking. International relations should not be about war, but about multinational information-sharing and sense-making.[24]

As far as the effectiveness of the intelligence garnered at the top of traditional Epoch-A hierarchies, the following quote from Daniel Ellsberg lecturing Henry Kissinger in the White House after Ellsberg's return from Viet-Nam is instructive; it refers to leadership's blind faith in the value of its narrow and often incorrect secret information:

> The danger is, you'll become like a moron. You'll become incapable of learning from most people in the world, no matter how much experience they have in their particular areas that may be much greater than yours.[25]

This ineffectiveness does not apply only to governments with an obsession for secrecy above integrity. It also applies to corporations. Here is a companion quote, this time from Ben Gilad, one of the top pioneers and practitioners of commercial intelligence:

> Top managers' information is invariably either biased, subjective, filtered or late . . . Using intelligence correctly requires a fundamental change in the way top executives make decisions.[26]

Another major difference is that Epoch A (the industrial era) tends to be unilateral in nature and non-consultative, much as the British and then the U.S. "empires" have been, and empires before them. Epoch B, in sharp contrast, is multilateral and collaborative in every sense of the word. This means that no history, no perspective, is excluded, with the result that more broadly beneficial and sustainable decisions are reached, grounded in the collective intelligence of the group. Because Epoch B is the information era, we are developing a network capable of connecting all individuals to all information all the time, which has the potential to strip the power from "rule by secrecy" hierarchies. Ultimately, this new operating system will be more effective and efficient, serving all. It will also be autonomous[27] from governments and corporations, now that the Arab Spring and specific incidents of misbehavior (e.g., PayPal cutting off WikiLeaks without due process) and legislative insanity (e.g., the Stop Online Privacy Act, a corrupt proposition exceeded only by the Supreme Court decision in "Citizens United") have demonstrated the absolute requirement for a public autonomous Internet.[28]

I now realize that neither governments nor corporations are "fixed" obstacles. In a world of constantly changing information, it is impossible for any structured organization to dominate a larger network—a hybrid network. Such broad, flexible governance without governments being "in charge" is where we need to go.[29] The objective: to implement transparency, truth, and trust across all boundaries.

David Weinberger[30] is a genius on this point: not only can no one person or even one organization or one country "know" what they need to know to make an informed decision, but if they fail to understand, respect, and "jack in" to the knowledge network with full transparency as the method and truth as the objective, they will make very bad decisions. Of course this does not address the issue of corruption, and the raw fact that most governments and corporations could care less about objective truths, seeking instead to optimize profits for the few at the expense of the many, but their ignorance is our advantage. That is why We the People must recommit ourselves to Open-Source Everything, its underpinnings (transparency and truth), and its outcome: trust you can bank on without a bank.

I will say that again in a different way: the persistent unethical and ignorant emphasis on secrecy and on making decisions for partisan advantage or to pay off campaign contributors and select insiders is not sustainable. We the People have an opportunity to embrace this manifesto of Open-Source Everything and *bury* "rule by secrecy." This is this is why I am optimistic about the future.

New, open-source, populist-based, information-era strategies will also serve our increasingly complex lives better in future situations of crisis such as natural disaster, war, and social disintegration. Collapse is cultural, systemic, a failure of process, not of any discrete event, institution, or location. The industrial-era model of command and control cannot adequately process information for a complex system, but an information-era model of distributed localized resilience can.

Collaboration and consensus is the Epoch-B way, but from the philanthropic foundations to the non-governmental organizations to all others, there is still a dearth of

14

information-sharing that is both expensive and incapacitating. While the United Nations has committed itself to coherence, with the meme of "Delivering as One," they do not have the intelligence—or the integrity—to actually do that. Similarly, governments talk of "whole of government" operations, and corporations of "matrixed management," but these also fail the intelligence and integrity tests.

Much has been written about how mass collaboration—alternatively called Collective Intelligence, Smart Mobs, Wisdom of the Crowds, Army of Davids[31]—has not been possible in complex situations in the past because the industrial era introduced (imposed) a cumulative series of information pathologies that deprived the group of access to all relevant information, while favoring an elite few with privileged access that allowed them to concentrate both power and wealth. In the public domain, many artificial—that is to say, contrived—obstacles to informing the public emerged in the past century, such as the following, each a book title:

Fog Facts.[32] These are facts that are "known" to some and publicly accessible but only if you know where to look. The mainstream media "blacks out" this knowledge. Modern examples include U.S. government support for dictators and U.S. government tolerance of massive fraud, waste, and abuse in return for fractional campaign contributions to presidential and legislative candidates who strive to remain in office "at any cost."

Forbidden Knowledge. This includes both knowledge forbidden for public consumption by governments (e.g., restrictions on pornography) as well as corporations (e.g., concealment of known pathologies such as the effect of tobacco on cancer, or toxins associated with household goods) and religions (the triumph of dogma over consciousness).

Lost History.[33] The most prominent modern example is the deliberate classification as secret of clandestine and covert operations by the U.S. government such that a modern history of foreign relations cannot be written—this is the documented complaint of the historians responsible for this task on behalf of the Department of State.[34] The role of the Central Intelligence Agency in the introduction of massive amounts of cocaine into the USA under the pretext of supporting "strategic" operations "at any cost" is especially frightening to anyone upholding the Constitution.[35]

Manufacturing Consent.[36] Noam Chomsky and Edward Herman first discussed this aspect of a modern democracy, and now, decades later, their work has been updated by Sheldon Wolin in his book, *Democracy Incorporated: Managed Democracy and the Specter of Inverted Totalitarianism.*[37] Corporations now "own" not just the legislative and executive branches of the U.S. government, but the judiciary as well, with the Supreme Court ruling on Citizens United being the more reprehensible evidence of the corruption of the highest court in the nation.

Missing Information.[38] Bill McKibben did something never done before—he recorded all the television channels being broadcast in his area in one twenty-four-hour period, and watched them all over the course of time. He then spent twenty-four hours alone in the wilderness. Comparing the two experiences, he produced a truly brilliant exposition of how much "missing information" there is in our lives.

Propaganda.[39] Propaganda, put most simply, is the development of manipulated (i.e., not truthful) information and the delivery of that information to an audience in such a way as to impress upon them views and beliefs that are not rooted in fact or deliberative dialog. Propaganda, which includes advertising that itself fosters an appreciation for planned obsolescence, waste, and toxic foods and goods, is the antithesis of transparency, truth, and trust.

Rule by Secrecy.[40] As we have all now realized, and as Occupy is now confronting on Wall Street and around the world, secret banking networks, not governments, have been making decisions about war and peace, poverty and prosperity. It is banks that profit most from wars, followed by the Military-Industrial-Congressional Complex, and We the People that suffer most. Government secrecy enables massive lies—such as the 935 documented lies[41] delivered by Dick Cheney that took us into a multi-trillion dollar losing war in Iraq[42]—and this is one reason why I have committed the balance of my life to Open-Source Everything: transparency, truth, and trust are the true currency for human transactions, and everything else is a cancer.

Weapons of Mass Deception.[43] Whereas Rule by Secrecy is about secret cabals making decisions on the truth as they know it, Weapons of Mass Deception are about blatant

THE OPEN-SOURCE EVERYTHING MANIFESTO

lies—many of them allowed to go unchallenged by the media, think tanks, university specialists, and all others who should be thinking in the public interest but instead choose to "go along" out of a selfish and unethical dependency on funding from the government doing the lying. A form of mass hysteria is achieved, one best illuminated by the manner in which the three singers of the band Dixie Chicks were treated when they publicly protested and questioned the veracity of the White House.[44] Now, years later, as with Jane Fonda on Viet-Nam, we know that the White House was committing treason, and the Dixie Chicks were both ethical and correct in their protestations. Mass hysteria—and mainstream media corruption—prevented the broader public from recognizing the truth at the time.

Weapons of Mass Instruction.[45] Underlying the ability of a treasonous White House and a complicit Congress (which must abdicate its Article 1 responsibilities when going along with known lies to permit an undeclared war at great cost) is a national educational system that is at best mediocre and at worst a crime against humanity. We are imposing on children of the Internet era—digital natives—an industrial-era system that is mindless: rote learning of old knowledge, sitting silent for hours on end, listening to lectures best left silent and so easily replaced by more vibrant multimedia communications. Teachers and the educational stakeholders who are complicit in the criminally negligent continuation of a retarded educational system are a foundation for an uninformed, unengaged public.[46]

Occupy as a meme and as a movement is challenging the status quo. So are Ron Paul, the Tea Party, the increasing numbers of Independents, and now the more active of the excluded political parties denied ballot access by the two-party tyranny: the Constitution Party, the Green Party, the Libertarian Party, and the Reform Party.

Now here is what they are *not* doing: getting a grip on public intelligence in the public interest. Of all the excluded parties, only the Green Party has a coherent set of core values and a truly distinguished coherent platform that sets forth its objectives. It does not have the capacity to challenge the factual platform of the incumbent Democratic president and his Cabinet, or the diverse Republican challengers among whom only Ron Paul is ethical and consistent. All candidates tend to lack intelligence or integrity to one degree or another—only a candidate willing to demand Electoral Reform, to announce a Coalition Cabinet and Balanced Budget plan in advance of the election, and able to commit to True-Cost Economics as pioneered by Herman Daly and others, is credible as a holistic candidate with intelligence and integrity.

To challenge those in power—and to win over those who have been sitting on the sidelines (half of the eligible voters do not vote) or "going along" with ideological idiocy whether from the extreme left or the extreme right (the other half)—the Third Wave must integrate public intelligence, public policy, and public participatory budgeting so as to demonstrate that We the People can not only self-govern, but we can reconstitute the "center" by mobilizing sixty percent of the eligible voters. (Since only half vote, that means mobilizing the other half, and out of the total, pulling in sixty percent to displace the two-party tyranny.) Only when we have demonstrated that we can either reassert our control over or abolish the government that is now a corporate neo-fascist plutocracy of, by, and for the one percent who have leveraged corruption to concentrate power and wealth will we be free again, and in all likelihood, prosperous as well.[47]

The corruption of all three branches of the federal government that has enabled the exclusion by the one percent of the ninety-nine percent from the very fruits that the Preamble of the Constitution states are the purpose of our government is at a minimum a total breach of the public trust, and at worst, treason and a crime against humanity.

> We the People of the United States, in order to form a more perfect Union, establish Justice, insure domestic Tranquility, provide for the common defence, promote the general Welfare, and secure the Blessings of Liberty to ourselves and our Posterity, do ordain and establish this Constitution for the United States of America.

I contend that the open-source approach is consistent with the direction in which our Founding Fathers intended this nation to develop, with liberty and a sovereign people, not "subjects," and also the direction in which societies want to go today. Evidence includes the fact that Occupy is a global movement, and the Arab Spring, like the freedom movements in the former Soviet

Union, is a regional uprising of people against corrupt and repressive governments.[48]

What the Founding Fathers did not articulate is the fact that sharing and the shared task of sense-making are what empowers the collective. It is not enough for the individual citizen to be smart or even good-hearted. They must be smart as a whole, a point made very ably by David Weinberger in *Too Big to Know: Rethinking Knowledge Now That the Facts Aren't the Facts, Experts Are Everywhere, and the Smartest Person in the Room Is the Room.*[49]

The contemporary challenge is our transition from the industrial-era worldview of unbridled consumption, selfishness, and "anything goes" to a new information-era worldview of "it's all connected," which means that we are all accountable for the whole. Resources are limited, brain power is virtually infinite. Open-Source Everything is the meme, the mind-set, and the method.

Today we are striving to both recreate the cohesive communities of the past, and to create a completely new discipline of intelligence (decision-support), one that elevates multinational collaboration and information-sharing to a much higher level. Multinational, Multiagency, Multi-disciplinary, Multidomain Information-Sharing and Sense-Making (M4IS2) originated as a Swedish military concept focused on the multinational aspects; I added the information aspects. Eventually, given an investment in M4IS2 and a demonstration of its power to lower costs and increase both peace and prosperity, we should be able to create the "Web 4.0 World Brain" and eradicate poverty, infectious disease, and environmental degradation. By this I mean the following, all together:

1. Adopt a **Strategic Analytic Model** for focusing our attention, our information, our tools, and our deliberative dialog.[50]
2. Accept the **Ten High-Level Threats to Humanity** as a common starting point for what stands in the way of a prosperous world at peace.[51]
3. Accept the **Twelve Core Policies** as a common starting point for how we plan and execute public programs.[52]
4. **Accept M4IS2**—and particularly its rejection of secrecy and the hoarding of information—as the method by which we can voluntarily harmonize public spending and behavior.[53]
5. Recognize the **fragmented knowledge structures** we have today (see Figure 5).
6. Accept personal responsibility for being a **citizen intelligence "minuteman"** who is engaged at least at the local level and ideally at all levels from local to global.[54]
7. **Demand transparency and truth** from every person, every organization, every government. Consider this the modern information-era equivalent of the Golden Rule.

Ultimately, this is about reaching the culminating point for humanity's next stage of consciousness, what some call Panarchy, others the World Brain, Global Brain, Global Mind, or Web 4.0. This is about connecting all human minds, all information in all languages and mediums, all the time.

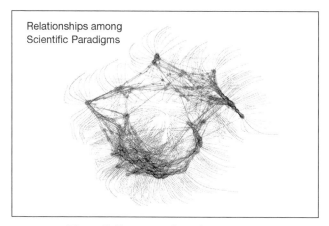

Figure 5: Fragmentation of Knowledge

Panarchy

Panarchy is an ideal condition in which every individual would be connected to all relevant information and able to participate in every decision of interest to them, from local to global. Panarchy thus represents direct democracy within a nonhierarchical, open-source context. In the ideal state of panarchy, every citizen is fully actualized, deeply steeped in integrity and intelligence, and able to participate creatively in the constant social reproduction of their world.[55]

Panarchy is a conceptual term coined in 1860 by Belgian botanist and economist Emie de Puydt. It refers to government, but a form of complete integrated governance that encompasses all other forms of organization. Other terms coined in this timeframe include "ecology," referring to an integrated system of living things, with the term "synergy" eventually specifying that individualism in isolation was insufficient to survival—the whole is greater than the sum of the parts, the whole has a tangible value in and of itself. This is consistent with David Weinberger's latest investigations in which he finds that in a room full of experts, the greatest intelligence is to be found in the room, not in the individual experts.

Over time that idea has blended with bottom-up concepts of self-governance to integrate the right of the individual to be a participant in any and all forms of governance touching his or her life, be they formal legal structures or informal cultural conventions. This model of decision-making and dissemination of intelligence has huge implications for the agility of communities to face catastrophic change, supporting self-sufficiency and resilience. At its best, panarchy provides for near-perfect resilience in the face of great complexity because it reduces the resistance between all human minds and reaction points to near zero. What this means is every human mind is connected to every other human mind, and to all relevant information; that observations by any human immediately reach all other humans (imagine super-Twitter); and that with tools for thinking, the relevant human intelligence can be aggregated and applied to any situation in near-real time. This is not something corporations or governments can do today.

Open-Source Everything and panarchy are symbiotic— a state of being, a state of mind, a state of the Earth.

José Argüelles, following French mystic Teilhard de

Chardin and others, has defined the term *noosphere* as a "collectively experienced ego-free state," as well as a realm or "band" of equally accessible consciousness surrounding the Earth.[56] The organization of a planetary community based on panarchic principles could help bring about this noospheric condition by creating a society based on equals, where all have the same voice, the same freedom, and the same access to education. In other words, no corruption, no lies, no resistance. Only transparency, truth, and trust. Such an ideal condition of free being is, of course, threatening to those who believe that elite privilege and hierarchical domination are the only effective ways to organize and run technocratic civilization.

Panarchy is not linear—it is characterized by continuous cycles of growth (both evolution and mutation), accumulation, restructuring (including creative destruction), and renewal.

Both panarchy and resilience depend on good information and constant, rapid, truthful feedback loops at all points within each system and among systems. Panarchy focuses on the rights of the individual living being to be a part of the total communications environment—with voice and vote. Resilience is more of an outcome of panarchy, created when the feedback loops are so continuous, authentic, and truthful that they lead to early perception of problem areas, early consideration of alternative courses of action, and early reactions. In short, panarchy and resilience and innovation and systemic stability (not to be confused with *status quo*) are all related.

The deepest transformation that must take place is within each of us, as we all begin to insist on living life in panarchic form. We must each cast off our past indoctrination as cogs of little importance, and fulfill our promise as vibrant engaged beings who are capable of what Kevin Kelly and others have called "hive mind."[57]

Enter "Radical Man"

I'd like to introduce two graphics from the 1970s here, because the human is the heart of this story about the truth, and only the human can choose to be what Charles Hampden-Turner calls "Radical Man." In a book by that title,[58] the first theoretical thesis ever accepted at the Harvard Business School (against enormous opposition), he examined the fundamental role of the individual human being within capitalism, demonstrating that when the human is commoditized, capitalism fails; when the human is unleashed, capitalism benefits all.

Defining, perhaps for the first time, nine specific attributes of the "fully functional" human being (Perception, Identity, Competence, Investment, Suspension and Risk, Transcendence, Synergy, Integration, and Complexity), his work remains highly relevant to the broad movement seeking to achieve evolutionary consciousness.

Figure 6 illustrates "Man as Slave or Commodity," and in Figure 7 shows "Man as Free Spirit—Radical Man." This could not be more vital to our understanding of how to create a prosperous world at peace: the one inexhaustible resource and innovation source capable of rising to all challenges is the human brain. We billion rich have failed to create a prosperous world at peace—we must now do what we can to help the five billion poor connect, innovate, and sustain our Earth.

In sharp contrast, here is man operating at "full capacity."

The integrative work of Hampden-Turner shows how vitally important it is to humanity and to our various forms of enterprise for each person to be a free self rather than a weak or controlled slave (even a fabulously wealthy slave). The industrial era sentenced most men and women and children to lives as inert "cogs" in a system that denies their humanity, and in denying that humanity, represses

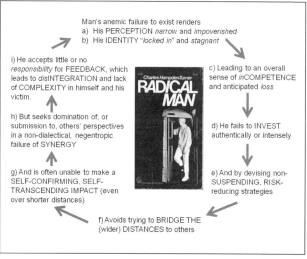

Man's anemic failure to exist renders
a) His PERCEPTION *narrow* and *impoverished*
b) His IDENTITY "*locked in*" and *stagnant*

i) He accepts little or no *responsibility* for FEEDBACK, which leads to *dis*INTEGRATION and lack of COMPLEXITY in himself and his victim.

c) Leading to an overall sense of *in*COMPETENCE and anticipated *loss*

h) But seeks domination of, or submission to, others' perspectives in a non-dialectical, negentropic failure of SYNERGY

d) He fails to INVEST authentically or intensely

g) And is often unable to make a SELF-CONFIRMING, SELF-TRANSCENDING IMPACT (even over shorter distances)

e) And by devising non-SUSPENDING, RISK-reducing strategies

f) Avoids trying to BRIDGE THE (wider) DISTANCES to others

Charles Hampden-Turner
RADICAL MAN

Figure 6: Man as Slave or Commodity

the very God-given or cosmos-inherent capacities that we alone among all the beasts on the planet possess: the capacity to innovate and create beyond any individual's wildest imagination, but working together in the aggregate, using shared information and collective sense-making as a foundation for eradicating waste and achieving optimal harmonious wealth creation for all.

The similarity of the cycles of panarchy, nature, and life itself with creation, growth, conservation, and then rebirth is notable. In the first Hampden-Turner figure, man is dormant, waiting; in the second man is authentic, engaged, creative, and a full participant in the complexity that is humanity on Earth.

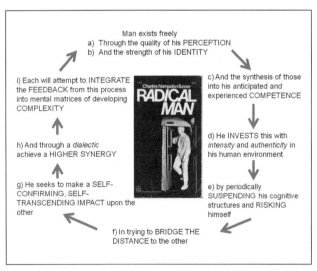

Man exists freely
a) Through the quality of his PERCEPTION
b) And the strength of his IDENTITY

i) Each will attempt to INTEGRATE the FEEDBACK from this process into mental matrices of developing COMPLEXITY

c) And the synthesis of those into his anticipated and experienced COMPETENCE

h) And through a *dialectic* achieve a HIGHER SYNERGY

d) He INVESTS this with *intensity* and *authenticity* in his human environment

g) He seeks to make a SELF-CONFIRMING, SELF-TRANSCENDING IMPACT upon the other

e) by periodically SUSPENDING his cognitive structures and RISKING himself

f) In trying to BRIDGE THE DISTANCE to the other

Figure 7: Man as Free Spirit—Radical Man

In my view, the many spiritual movements that seek to expand human consciousness and foster a sense of community have failed in one vital respect: they have not focused on the urgency of putting humans in touch with real-world information, not just "themselves."

Open-Source Everything is about creating a World Brain and Global Game in which all humans play themselves, have access to all other humans and all relevant information, and therefore, as free spirits, are self-governing in concert with all others, using shared information as the means for voluntarily and peacefully harmonizing behavior and investment at all levels to achieve a world that works for all.

Public intelligence in the public interest. That is the missing ingredient.

Terms of Reference

Sustainable resilient civilization is achievable, and the balance of this book discusses the specific strategy and tactics of achieving panarchy through Open-Source Everything. First, however, a few terms merit definition.

Integrity represents holistic completeness. In an integral system, all the dots are connected, and each node in the network has access to the complete knowledge of the whole, much as the synapses in our brain are interconnected through a holographic orchestration. On the level of government and the state, this means that the position of the citizen trumps the status of the government employee—in other words, holarchy supplants hierarchy.

Holarchy is a term coined by Arthur Koestler, a combination of the Greek word *holos* meaning "whole," and the generally understood word "hierarchy." It treats every individual as both an individual and a vital part of a whole. Holoarchy has always been "reality," but in our rush to implement the emergent concepts of the industrial era, we exceeded our understanding in adopting a "command and control" approach, a top-down "because I said so" approach that created a separation between "elites" and "all others." Holarchy is the Epoch-B concept for self-governance within the whole.

Hierarchy is the Epoch-A approach to organization, in which everything from armies to religions has been organized in a top-to-bottom structure where rank matters more than knowledge, and the approach to knowledge is arrogant and insular—an assumption that being at the top implies nearly-divine powers, and certainly absolute authority over all that is "below." As we can now see with the example of the U.S. government, including the corruption of Congress and the Executive branch and the Courts, and the massive financial fraud that was enabled by that corruption, the fact is that elites are ignorant, isolated, and not to be trusted. In the absence of the knowledge of the whole (the "hive mind"), elites thrive at everyone else's expense.

This latter point is very important because too many senior executives and our most senior uniformed officers (the four-star generals and admirals) in the U.S. government have been "going along" with impeachable offenses by political decision-makers because they confused loyalty to the chain of command with what should have been their only loyalty: to the citizens they serve and the legitimacy of the whole, which is founded on truth as well as service to the Constitution that they swear an oath to protect and defend. Lacking in integrity in the fullest sense of the word, these people in power of course also fail all those larger communities to which they have an implied responsibility—Earth, for example.

Intelligence. The purpose of intelligence-gathering is to support accurate decision-making. In no way should "intelligence" be confused with secrecy. The proper role of intelligence-gathering (providing support for good decisions to be made) goes back to ancient times, but it is not well practiced by bureaucracies that use secrecy to escape accountability. As a process and a function, the collection of intelligence includes some very specific elements and capabilities that can—and should be—applied in the Open-Source Everything spirit:

1. *Requirements definition.* Intelligence is decision-support—this means that a decision is required in which trade-offs have to be evaluated. If there are no trade-offs, there is no real decision. The questions have to be asked: What do you need to know? To what end? When? In what form? When serving larger community

31

groups, it is especially important to help them understand what they know, what they do not know, and what they need to know.

2. *Collection management.* The biggest reason spies fail is because they only understand secret sources and methods. They are simply not serious about appreciating all that can be known legally and ethically through open sources. At the same time, in the private sector the craft of intelligence is not well-developed. Even the energy and the pharmaceutical companies—the very best in the business—lack the integrity to actually think through the sustainable economics and the holistic health alternatives. The acme of skill in collection management is to know who knows; to know what sources are likely to be most relevant and cost-effective; and to know how to determine and cope with inherent biases, a different bias within each source.

3. *Source discovery and validation.* As stunning as it may sound, neither spies nor the private sector are as good as they should be about discovering all the human sources, all the analog sources, and all the digital sources relevant to their inquiry. In the past the "true costs" have been ignored, hidden, or externalized to the public. One of the most interesting aspects of crowd-sourcing (openly soliciting and appreciating contributions from everyone and anyone, instead of a narrow, pre-selected group of experts—a crucial part of Open-Source Everything) is that it harnesses the distributed intelligence—the distributed eyes, ears,

senses—of all human minds all the time. "Put enough eyeballs on it," and not only is no bug invisible, but neither is any fact of corruption nor any relevant bit of information.

4. *Information integration.* This intelligence capability can be harnessed with ease or difficulty, but if you are organized such that information is hoarded as a source of (old) power, then the task is virtually impossible. This is how all governments and corporations from the industrial era are organized. Sadly, secret intelligence agencies not only distinguish among Confidential, Secret, and Top Secret, they also "compartment" information into smaller communities of access. What this really means is that no one, ever, gets the whole picture, even when working only with secrets from all secret sources. Combine that with the fact that outside the secret world there is no substantive appreciation for the craft of intelligence (decision-support), and you have the root problem of the human race today: we have forgotten our history, have no idea of our present, and have given up our future.

5. *Analytics.* The craft of analysis is a mix of art and science poorly understood in the domains of education, intelligence, and research. Analytics mixes the best of what machines can do (very large data processing to find patterns and anomalies difficult for individual humans to achieve) and the best of what humans can do (intuitive leaps of the imagination that no machine can accomplish).

6. *Visualization and presentation.* Visualization is also an art and science, combining deep knowledge of the subject matter with deep knowledge of the possibilities for concise, coherent, as well as compelling, actionable, timely presentation of the product of this process—intelligence—to the deciding person or group.

7. *Feedback.* This completes the "loop" such that there is continuous interactive relation among all those who are engaged in the craft of intelligence.

As we all become more familiar with the concept of "true cost," using public intelligence to factor in all the costs that governments and corporations have learned to externalize to the public—water and electricity costs, pollution and other environmental costs, child labor costs, tax avoidance costs, to name a few—we are better able to demand complete integrity from others *and* offer it up ourselves. Integrity and intelligence at all levels across all topics are pre-conditions for creating a prosperous world at peace, for the simple reason that today corruption—a lack of integrity and a lack of intelligence—is consuming fifty percent of every dollar across defense, energy, health, and intelligence, to name just four high-cost domains.[59]

CHAPTER 2

Open-Source Everything

Despite decades of reading, it was not until recently, when I read Charles Eisenstein's *Sacred Economics: Money, Gift, and Society in the Age of Transition,*[1] that I made the connection between traditional gift and sharing societies, and the current modern interest in Open-Source Everything within and among the various counterculture elements of society.

The example that author used, that of child care, is compelling. In traditional societies, child care is inherent in the community, where all adults accept a responsibility for all children. Child care is, in other words, both "free" and of very high nurturing value. In modern society, where the time of all humans has been commoditized, child care is made "scarce"—it has become a "good" that must be purchased. The spiritual "cost" of this change is only now being understood by a growing number of humans interested in restoring resilient communities that are both spiritual and sustainable.

Although I have been a proponent of open-source intelligence and evolved into being a proponent of open-source everything, I had not made the deeper connection that is elucidated so well in *Sacred Economics* between the "root" nature of humanity and Earth as "open" (connected and freely giving/exchanging) and the toxic, near-fatal nature of what we have today: banks, corporations, and governments that by being "closed" represent the death of humanity from "rule by secrecy" (however morally good the people working in these structures may be as individuals).

Others have written about the "fencing of the commons" and I recommend that entire body of literature. In pre-industrial civilization the concept of private property did not apply to Mother Earth—the land, the sea and the waterways, the air, sunlight could not be "owned," only shared and nurtured in stewardship.

When we allowed for the "taking" of Earth resources for private profit, without regard to the true cost of the taking to the ninety-nine percent as well as future generations, we broke the Whole Earth System, literally. We began corrupting the smooth feedback loops and ecologies that had been centuries in the making, in essence poking holes in the fabric of nature within which man had been a component, but not a dominant nor even a decisive change agent.

Free/Open-Source Software

Free software, of which Richard Stallman is the recognized modern champion, was pioneered by IBM with its releases of operating system software in the 1950s and 1960s, and the associated SHARE, Inc., volunteer organization that maintained the software library and aggregated user experiences. In September 1983, Stallman launched the GNU (as in Good Not Unix) Project to create a free (openly available source code, not free of charge) operating system intended to displace Unix. This is widely credited with being the beginning of the free software movement; in 1985 he founded the Free Software Foundation.

Stallman's brilliance and enduring contribution was the creation of a coherent mix of free software, the concept of copyleft (access is free, only financial profit is constrained), and the process for collaborative development and enhancement of software by volunteers.

In January 1998 a handful of members of the free-software movement met in Palo Alto, California, to discuss how best to announce the release of source code for Navigator. It was at this point that a consensus emerged about a need to break from the unintended intellectual implications of "free," i.e., free of cost. The heart of F/OSS is not in avoiding financial costs, but rather in avoiding opportunity costs imposed by proprietary or concealed source code that cannot be improved upon by others at will.

As related in Wikipedia (Open-Source/History), citing Michael Tiermann's "History of the Open-Source Initiative," it was Christine Peterson who suggested "Open Source" to the others, including Todd Anderson, Larry Augustin, Jon Hall, Sam Ockman, Michael Tiermann, and Eric S. Raymond. Over the next week, Raymond and others worked on spreading the word. Linus Torvalds gave an all-important sanction the following day. Richard Stallman chose to reject the term.

That same year the linguistic, intellectual, and philosophical discordance between "free" and "open source" came to a head at the Freeware Summit organized by Tim O'Reilly. Those favoring the term "open source" over "free" were pointing out that access to the code, not free of cost, is the core requirement. In a classic demonstration of the power of open-source culture, all present discussed, voted, and adopted "open source" as the preferred alternative. The Open-Source Initiative was then established, today led by Michael Tiermann. Below is the mission statement of this very important initiative:

> *The Open-Source Initiative (OSI) is a non-profit corporation with global scope formed to educate about and advocate for the benefits of Open-Source and to build bridges among different constituencies in the Open-Source community.*
>
> *Open-Source is a development method for software that harnesses the power of distributed peer review and transparency of process. The promise of Open-Source is better quality, higher reliability, more flexibility, lower cost, and an end to predatory vendor lock-in.*[2]

Properly and ethically understood, the term "open-source software" refers to the complete availability of all relevant source code for public scrutiny and enhancement. This does not mean that the software must be free of charge. It does mean that those vendors who make only portions of their software available and then seek to label all their software "open source" are committing fraud.

At root, F/OSS is about preventing governments and corporations from concealed functionality (the ability to access your data and do other things without your

permission and without your knowing), and from imposing financial costs and inefficiencies (such as very badly
written code that consumes hardware and energy and
time) on the individual citizen. In India, Stallman suc-
ceeded in persuading the government to dispense with
Microsoft products across the entire university system,
using instead F/OSS. Not only have the financial savings
been enormous, the constantly improving open-source
software renders huge enhancements in human produc-
tivity not possible with Microsoft's somewhat retarded
combinations of capabilities.

Open-Source Hardware and More

Open-Source Hardware is a direct spin-off of the Open-
Source Software movement. As with software, but now in
the realm of the physical, it evolves through collaboration
and the use of open specifications, standards, and other
freely shared details necessary to create all manner of
computer-related hardware including mobile telephones,
micro-processors and processors, handheld computers in
their entirety, and now larger computing centers.

Although there is a broad range of open-source applications, three merit mention here: Open Data Access, Open
Spectrum, and Open Tools.

Open Data Access is an open framework that allows
digital data to be accessed by common applications, which
is essential to scalable sharing. This is not to be confused
with Open Content, which refers to content licensed in

a manner that provides users with the right to utilize the content in more ways than those normally permitted under copyright, at no cost to the user.[3] For example, a professor is free to make copies for students, rather than paying a copyright fee for each individual copy of a paper. Open Data Access, in contrast, refers to digital accessibility.

Open Spectrum, pioneered by David Weinberger, is a revival of the ham radio culture, reinforced by the practical knowledge that radio and other atmospheric frequency spectrum allocation is very inefficient and often antithetical to the needs of society.[5] The sale of spectrum creates monopolies of use, the military's being the largest, and it encourages private-sector monopolies to rely on the exclusivity of their spectrum allocation rather than on innovation since assigned spectrum does not allow for the kind of scaling of a multiplicity of applications such as are emerging today. The consequences of this can be seen in Afghanistan, where drones, normal aviation, and normal communications are all in conflict in an intense environment, because for the past several decades no one has demanded that they each be able to operate in a shared-spectrum environment.

Finally, Open Tools, starting with open farm technologies—such as creating tractors and other mechanized tools with standardized inter-changeable parts that are easy to make and not subject to royalty fees, and much cheaper than complex machines offered for sale—led to Open-Source Ecology.[6] This network of farmers, engineers, and supporters is building the Global Village

Construction Set,[7] which aims to include fifty different industrial machines with open specifications and interchangeable parts—one of the most breathtaking revolutionary activist initiatives that I know about.

OpenMoko, the concept of a handheld device that integrates open-source software and open-source hardware, is alive and well. When combined with OpenBTS[8] and Open-Mesh Networks,[9] it is the cornerstone for empowering the five billion poor—simultaneously educating them "one cell call at a time" and unleashing their entrepreneurial energies, while also creating the Autonomous Internet, one that cannot be shut down by any government or corporation.

OpenBTS is the open-source software/hardware combination that replicates cellular phone services using open spectrum, enabling free and very low-cost communications. Combined with mesh networks and other means of disconnecting from the government/telecommunications monopoly of the grid, OpenBTS is the foundation "liberation technology" and is central to the release of humanity from corrupt hierarchies and their "rule by secrecy."

When the five billion poor receive OpenBTS and have access to the Internet, everything will change.

Open-Source Intelligence

Although Open-Source Intelligence is the best method for gathering accurate and timely information, nobody and no agency of the government is serious about collecting and analyzing it. Consider this quote from Ellen Siedman, former member of the President's National Economic Council:

> CIA reports only focus on foreign economic conditions. They don't do domestic economic conditions and so I cannot get a strategic analysis that compares and contrasts strengths and weaknesses of the industries I am responsible for. On the other hand, Treasury, Commerce, and the Fed are terrible at the business of intelligence—they don't *know* how to produce intelligence.[10]

Inspired by the open-source software revolution as I saw it, I came to the same conclusions as Anonymous and WikiLeaks: that the reliance by the U.S. government specifically, and all governments generally, on intelligence services that were obsessed with secret sources and methods, and oblivious to open source and its methods, were costing the taxpayer a great deal of money to very little effect.

My focus increasingly became the more open, ethical, legal alternative of creating public intelligence in the public interest. It was not hard to recognize, as an intelligence professional, that a large part of the modern open-source revolution had to focus on tailored content—i.e., Open-Source Intelligence (OSINT).

I made one big mistake that haunts me to this day. Because I had not been fully radicalized, I still believed, from 1988 to 2006, that governments were the center of gravity for achieving my vision, and that I should devote myself to helping governments get a grip on open sources of information.

The Aspin-Brown Report, more formally known as the Commission on the Roles and Capabilities of the U.S. Intelligence Community, stated in its final report that OSINT should become a top priority of the Director of Central Intelligence (DCI), and also a top priority for funding. This finding was a result of my testimony to the Commission (an exercise in which I beat the entire secret world on a challenge to report in a matter of days on Burundi, detailed in the Epilogue) and a subsequent internal staff investigation. I mistakenly believed that I had made my point at the highest possible levels and with the greatest possible effect, but a succession of directors have refused to attend to any of the Aspin-Brown recommendations, including this one.

In 1996 the DCI, then George Tenet, ordered a special study to determine what would be needed to cover for the president all the topics not properly covered by the secret world with its obsession on secrets. In June 1997 he received the report, created by Boyd Sutton, entitled "The Challenge of Global Coverage."[11] To the DCI's surprise, the report recommended a $1.5 billion annual investment in open sources of information, calculated at $10 million a year for each of 150 countries and issues not addressed by a system focused on seven "hard target" countries led by China and Russia. Tenet ordered the study locked up and disregarded, not to be spoken of again. However, being unclassified in draft form, the study found its way into the open and can be read online. It is an indictment of the U.S. secret intelligence community for its persistent failure—despite entreaties from multiple stakeholders—to be responsible for "global coverage."

On July 22, 2004, the 9/11 Commission issued its final report, which included mentions on pages 23 and 423 of a new national Open-Source Agency separate from the CIA.[12] Since then, and based in large part on the deliberate recommendations of the Aspin-Brown and 9/11 Commission reports, senior executives in the Office of Management and Budget have twice approved the establishment of an Open-Source Agency, with a first-year budget of $125 million, and a final target budget of at least $2 billion.[13]

The agency was never established, due to enormous hostility and opposition from the secret world, and the lack of a Cabinet-level champion for the Open-Source Agency.[14] The Secretary of State would be the obvious natural leader for this proposed agency based fully in our democratic tradition and ideally suited as an engine for creating both a "Smart Nation" and a global multinational information-sharing and sense-making capability. Such an agency could help address high-level threats to humanity, in part by harmonizing how all stakeholders (not just governments) spend money across the many policy domains and political boundaries.

I have tried several times to inform Hillary Clinton, Secretary of State since 2008, about this, at one point enlisting Lawrence Lessig, with the help of Michael Tiermann (President of the Open-Source Initiative), to communicate the opportunity to Alec Ross in the Office of the Undersecretary of State for Policy. I have no direct knowledge, but I speculate that the secret world intimidated Alec Ross and frightened him away from talking to me, because they know that the day an Open-Source Agency is fully operational, the President and Congress will be able to cut the secret budget by two thirds.[15]

These suggestions about implementing open-source strategies constitute my practical approach to contributing to the transformation of the Republic and the larger community of humankind. It is my personal and professional belief—as someone deeply concerned about both security and intelligence—that security can only be attained through pure transparency not secrecy. Intelligence can only be maximally effective if it is open and collective. At present, the contrast between the secret intelligence community and the alternative open-source intelligence community could not be starker. This illustrates the failure of banks, corporations, government, and non-governmental organizations (such as global charities, with the Red Cross coming to mind) to act purely in the public interest. There are two reasons for this: one, because they can hide behind secrecy and not be accountable for some or all of their acts; and two, because in the absence of public intelligence, the public is impotent.

The Open-Source Pyramid in Detail

Since the development of F/OSS in the 1980s and 1990s, and the globalization of open-source intelligence, the meme has spread. Today there is a plethora of open-source movements and endeavors—but no one has brought them together. This manifesto seeks both to expand the open-source revolution and make it the central enabler for creating a prosperous world at peace.

On the next few pages I list a wide range of "opens" within each of the layers illustrated in the Open-Source Pyramid (Figure 1), simply to illuminate the wide-ranging, near-universal nature of this meme. This is not a complete list![16] The order below corresponds to Figure 1.

Aspects

Open Access. Generally legal right to view, read, transit.

Participation. Generally open right to contribute or utilize.

Transparency. General visibility of detail to any who wish access.

Shareability/Forkability. Peer property, sharing economy.

Enablers

Open-Access Publishing. Unrestricted public access.

Open Code. Excludes controlling or restrictive functions.[17]

Open Communication. Open access to communications net.

Open Data. Allows data to be integrated and exploited by all.

Open-Data Protocol. Web protocol for querying and updating.

Open Definition. Reuse/redistribute without technical limits.

Open Facilitation. Open-Space Technology (Harrison Owen).

Open Governance.[18] Panarchy,[19] sociocracy,[20] holacracy.[21]

Open Licenses. Creative Commons is an example.

Open Standards. W3C[22] is an example.

Infrastructure (Physical)

Open-Source Food. Transparency of the food-supply chain.

Open-Source Agriculture. Open DNA[23] and biotechnology.

Open Global Village Construction Set. Actual generic tools.

Open Cloud. Open standards, ease of mix and match.[24]

Open-Collaboration Platform. Technical, e.g., Wiki.

Open-Collaboration Spaces. Hacker spaces, e.g., HackLabs.

Open-Data Grid. Project underway to enhance data storage.

Open Funding. Crowd-sourcing, social lending.

Open Manufacturing. Open software creating the physical world.

Open Media. Video, audio, and text that can be shared freely.

Open Meeting. Organizational meeting open
to the public.
Open Mobile. Standards and unlocked devices.
Open Spectrum. Unlicensed spectrum shared by all.
Open Territories. Regions committed to the open
meme.

Practices

Open Knowledge and Science. Open Knowledge
Foundation.
Open and Free Software. LINUX, Ubunto, Debian, etc.
Open Designs. Demotech, Howtopedia, Instructables.
Open Currencies or Money. BitCoin, OpenCoin, etc.
Open Funding. Crowd-sourcing, social lending.
Open Capital. B2B sharing of risk and reward.
Open Hardware. Arduino, Buglabs, OpenMoko.

Domains

Open Education. Open Accreditation, Connectivist
Learning.
Open Science. Cambia, Bios, BioBrick.
Open Government and Open Politics. Sunlight
Foundation.
Open Business. Integration of buyers and suppliers.
Open Skies. National agreements to enable
transparency.
Open Spirituality. Anabaptism,[25] Reiki,[26] Yoga.[27]

Products

Open Courseware. Freely available online
  (but not credits).
Open Government Data. Funded by taxpayer,
  open to public.
Open Journals. Free public access to archives.
Open Textbooks. Free public access, deliberately
  organized.
Open Tools. Mix and match, modular, affordable.

Movements

Open Coalition. Emerging non-partisan grassroots
  concept.
Open Materials. Enable do-it-yourself (DIY)
  production.

Consciousness

Open Spirituality. Integrates open, participatory,
  commons.

Michel Bauwens, founder of the P2P Foundation, is a
gifted author able to envision and explain the emergence
and the potential end state of Open-Source Everything.
He says:

> . . . as modernity was about rigorously individualising
> everything, eventually reaching the current dead-end
> of hyper-individualism, we are now just as rigorously
> 'relationising' everything . . . (T)he three paradigm
> shifts (open/free, participatory, commons), although

only emerging as seed forms at this stage, are letting themselves be felt through contemporary spiritual practices.[28]

Bauwens is touching on what I have long considered the duality of spiritual practice: on the one hand, focusing very successfully on reconnecting individuals to one another; on the other, ignoring the proven process of intelligence, a process that connects minds to facts.

"Open Everything" *is* everything—it is our mind, our heart, our soul, our destiny. In the next chapter I outline a summary manifesto for public consideration.

CHAPTER 3

Manifesto

The circumstances underlying this manifesto are stark and compelling: We are at the end of a five-thousand-year-plus historical process during which human society grew in scale while it abandoned the early indigenous wisdom councils and communal decision-making. Power was centralized in the hands of increasingly specialized "elites" and "experts" who not only failed to achieve all they promised but used secrecy and the control of information to deceive the public into allowing them to retain power over community resources that they ultimately looted.

In the beginning, there was the commons. Over vast stretches of prehistoric time, tribal cultures evolved in tandem with the natural environment. They did this without creating private property or hierarchical relationships of control and dominance that led to consumption of nature as a resource. Open-source culture provided for community sharing and community development. With the rise of patriarchy, empire, and systems of egoic control and empowerment, this open-source approach to community was destroyed. Over the course of the last centuries, the commons was fenced, and everything from agriculture to water was commoditized without regard to the true cost in non-renewable resources. Human beings, who had spent centuries evolving away from slavery, were re-commoditized by the Industrial Era.

The corruption of the commons led to the loss of integrity between and among individuals, organizations, and community. Artificial paradises made up of objects and possessions were substituted for true community based on authentic heart-to-heart relationships. Secular corruption is made possible by information asymmetries between those in power and the public. In the absence of transparency, truth, and trust, wealth is concentrated and waste is rampant.

We, *Homo sapiens*, are defined by what we know in the context of the Cosmos and the Earth—larger Whole Systems.

We, *Home sapiens*, were in harmony with the Cosmos and the Earth during earlier centuries when indigenous wisdom prevailed. The evolution of social forms and technology toward ever-greater levels of complexity is part of our human development toward deeper consciousness and self-awareness. The technosphere, as José Argüelles and others have realized, is the necessary detour that takes us from the pristine biosphere to the psychically collectivized state of the noosphere.

We live in a constellation of complex systems. It is impossible for any single person or even any single organization or nation in isolation to understand complex systems.

Collective intelligence—multinational, multiagency, multidisciplinary, multidomain information-sharing and sense-making—is the only means of obtaining near-real-time understanding of complex systems sufficient to achieve resilience in the face of changes. Many of these changes, including biospheric ones such as climate change and depletion of planetary resources, are the result of human activity and industry in the last three centuries.

As our technological capacities continue to increase and our environment becomes ever more fragile and endangered, we find that changes to the Earth that used to take ten thousand years now take a fraction of that. We must rediscover and reintegrate indigenous wisdom in order to come back into harmony with larger whole systems, and do so in a manner that allows for application of appropriate technologies and science, open-source intelligence gathering, and real-time self-governance. This means that we cannot afford to address our complex world with industrial-era hierarchies in which information travels laboriously up the chain to the top, some elites deliberate—lacking much of the information they need, and often lacking ethics as well—and then micro-management instructions go back down. All this takes time, and the instructions are invariably wrong. Instead, we harness the intelligence at the edge of the network—at the point of impact—and the individual who is face to face with a problem in a microcosm is the tip of the human spear, able both to reach back to all other humans for assistance, and to act on behalf of all humans in the moment.

It is in this light that we must recognize that only a restoration of open-source culture, and all that enables across the full spectrum of open-source possibilities, can allow humanity to harness the distributed intelligence of the collective and create the equivalent of heaven on Earth—in other words, a world that works for all.

History is a narrative we construct and a tool we can shape. Our model of history has been corrupted by "information pathologies" that include weapons of distortion and deception; suppression of alternatives and repression of inconvenient knowledge; and manufactured consent, propaganda, secrecy, and outright ideologically justified lies that go unchallenged by most journalists and scholars.

Knowledge has fragmented due to academic specialization, which supports an elite culture of secrecy and allows for control of populations by the wealthy few, who maintain surveillance and information-gathering operations. The sciences are divorced from the humanities and from religions; disciplines are divorced from one another; within disciplines the sub-disciplines have become tiny cultures in isolation from all other knowledge clusters.

We find ourselves at the end of centuries of isolation and alienation. We are at the beginning of the Great Awakening. The evolution of social technologies and communications media appears to align with prophecies of indigenous cultures like the classic Maya, who looked toward our epoch as the end of one great cycle and the beginning of another. It's a window of opportunity for us, potentially the threshold of transformation of humanity into a new psychic collectivity, a new global civilization that can attain galactic citizenship. We have the potential to achieve a radical evolution and expansion of our consciousness as a species, once we put aside all lesser goals.

Sharing, not secrecy, is the means by which we realize such a lofty destiny as well as create infinite wealth. The wealth of networks, the wealth of knowledge, revolutionary wealth—all can create a nonzero[1] win-win Earth that works for one hundred percent of humanity. This is the "utopia" that Buckminster Fuller foresaw, now within our reach.

Context matters. Context creates coherence and restores the missing connections that the fragmentation of knowledge into academic specializations has caused. Economy needs to be reimagined in terms of a whole-systems approach—the "true costs" of human action need to be measured holistically, in terms of effects on the regenerative capacity of the biosphere as a whole. If we as *Homo sapiens* fail to connect the dots and make decisions on the basis of truthful, true-cost information, we will self-destruct.

Clarity (transparency) is the means by which we nurture the recognition and sharing of truth.

Diversity is how our human species will achieve ongoing abundance by liberating human innovation.

Integrity is how we enter into a "state of grace" and become "one with God," however you choose to define and understand these broad terms. This manifesto defines "God" as an experience of collective solidarity that extends from the human realm to the universe as a whole.

Sustainability can only be achieved through mass collaboration and the achievement of panarchy—a constellation of co-equal hybrid systems of self-governance in which all individuals freely choose where they wish to be heard, and have full access to all relevant information.

Culture is the soul of the community, the "glue" that keeps the lessons of history alive, that demands clarity, that unifies diversity, that nurtures and demands integrity, and thus sustains the community.

A model for public intelligence is proffered in this book, ideally providing a means for every citizen to be a collector, producer, and consumer of public intelligence (decision-support).

A model for informed democracy also is proffered here—it provides a means for achieving panarchy, enabling every citizen to have access to all relevant information and to participate constructively in an infinite number of self-selected communities of interest.

Organized people will defeat organized money every time. We must all come together to begin a new era that restores the sovereignty of the public in the aggregate over all other forms of organization and influence.

Panarchy is the end-state, Radical Man is the soul, Reflexive Practice is the process, and Web 4.0—all people connected to one another and all information in all languages all the time—is the means whereby we create and actualize a World Brain and Global Game, a *noosphere*, and achieve evolutionary collective consciousness.

The goal is to reject money and concentrated illicitly aggregated and largely phantom wealth in favor of community wealth defined by community knowledge, community sharing of information, and community definition of truth derived in transparency and authenticity, the latter being the ultimate arbiter of shared wealth.

When we relate and share knowledge authentically, this places us in a state of grace, a state of "win-win" harmony with all others, and establishes trust among all.

CHAPTER 4

Philosophical Concepts

Truth, Coin of Collective Consciousness

> When things are not going well, until you get the truth
> out on the table, no matter how ugly, you are not in a
> position to deal with it.
>
> —Bob Seelert[1]

Truth is the foundation for all discourse and wise decision-making. There is no such thing as truth in isolation. The definition of meaning is a contextual and communal process, as the following two statements[2] communicate succinctly:

Put enough eyeballs on it, no bug is invisible.

The truth at any cost lowers all other costs.

The first concept makes clear the role of community in arriving at the truth of any matter. The second makes clear the moral and financial value of truth, reducing all manner of costs across all domains including time and space. Neither of these concepts matter to the greedy, selfish one percent—they matter very much to the ninety-nine percent.

Our concept of truth becomes more universal as we reach higher levels of consciousness and awareness, taking in a wider spectrum of information and possibility. As we adapt a more expanded perspective on our reality, our concept of what is true and meaningful changes—from local to regional, regional to global, beyond global to the galaxy, and then to the cosmos. The evolution of our species and possibly the Earth depends upon the realization of an ever-expanding concept of truth. Anything less keeps us small, as Lawrence of Arabia is depicted to have said to Sherif Ali in the classic movie:

> Sherif Ali! So long as the Arabs fight community against community, so long will they be a little people, a silly people, greedy, barbarous and cruel, as you are.[3]

Most of us have lived in small groupings defined by accidents of geography and history. Over-identifying with our ethnic or national backgrounds, we have been these "little people." As we move into a world-centric perspective, we shed our over-identification with local and more parochial forms of thought. We seek universal truths and principles that are systemic and holistic rather than fragmented and subjective.

The truth is what one shares that one believes to be the case. It may not be true in an absolute or objective sense, but if one believes it to be true, one is not telling a lie or misrepresenting what he or she believes. Exchange of authentic perspective with openness to development and change of belief is the necessary beginning for any discourse that might lead to consensus and thus generate authentic knowledge. The scientific method, when it functions properly, allows truth to emerge via competing hypotheses—at least in the domain of what can be quantified and verified through repetition of an experimental procedure.

It is our obligation to speak of what we know as we know it, not dissembling or deceiving. This could be considered the "moral truth," and ultimately it is what can be validated by others so that a consensus can be arrived at and shared.

Many aspects of truth *can* be known—within the limits of individual human discernment and with the advantages that accrue from a collective endeavor (collective intelligence). The sharing of truth in the form of widely available information creates a foundation for cost-effective transparent decisions that are inherently anti-corrupt in nature. In the field of open-source intelligence, one could say that truth equals all the information critical to any subject, translated into any language, available all the time.

Where the philosophy gets interesting, even challenging, is when it confronts the reality that dogma, opinion, and deception can create in the mind a view of reality that is not real, but that one considers to be truthful. This gets to the heart of why education is the root requirement and right of each individual in any true democracy, and why democracy dies when dogma, ideology, and propaganda flourish. Truth is our best effort to see reality as it really is, and make the most of it. And please note that science, faith, and philosophy should not be considered antithetical to one another.

Truth does change, both in the mind of man and in the larger reality where man resides. On the one hand, advancing knowledge and paradigm shifts can render old truths sadly insufficient, while bringing forward new, more robust truths. At the same time, actions taken by man while operating under old truths (for example, assuming that the Corps of Engineers can pave over the Mississippi wetlands and levee the largest river in the continental U.S. without having a Katrina-like consequence) create new truths—severe weather events that are not an Act of God but rather an Act of Man acting very badly over time and space.

The truth in philosophy is nuanced. It is not just an intellectual truth that is recognized, but a spiritual and sensual one as well. Truth involves discerning moral values to live by. It appears to prosper when citizens are educated and enjoy civil liberties including freedom of expression.

The moral truth is worth dying for—sometimes a burning monk (Viet-Nam) or fruit vendor (Tunisia) is the catalyst needed to illuminate the culture of fear and lies such that the public reconnects to its own power to be the truth, to define the truth, to demand the truth. How we seek, sense, and share with one another is a function of, among many variables, one constant: whether we are in a state of grace such that the truth is the primary attribute of all that we see, smell, touch, and sense.

My own motto since the 1990s:

E Veritate Potens
From Truth, We (the People) Are Made Powerful[4]

Truth is one of the core philosophical concepts most applicable to open-source everything.

To address this concept I draw heavily on the wisdom of Will Durant, one of the greatest philosophers and historians in the English language. His 1916 doctoral thesis, *Philosophy and the Social Problem*,[5] and his life's work with his wife Ariel Durant, the eleven-volume *The Story of Civilization*,[6] remain unmatched. His emphasis on education and the resulting advance of humanity dovetails with the purposes of this manifesto in the sense that learning to discern and disseminate the truth is the ultimate role for any human.

Truth is the currency for collective consciousness, vital as a means of earning trust, which is itself a currency and a major factor in creating wealth within and among nations.

The philosophical reflections of many great thinkers help put the value and socio-cultural significance of "truth" in perspective. They frame the larger questions of who we are, how we wish to live, and how we relate to one another and to the challenges of our time. They also frame the role of truth in relation to the paranormal and the extraterrestrial, as well as the cosmic consciousness that could ultimately be where science, philosophy, religion, and ideally our individual existences become "One."

In *Philosophy and the Social Problem*, the "social problem" is that of keeping an entire public in harmony with its government, its private sector, and its divisions of ethnicity, gender, age, and education, among others. It is the problem of governance of the whole, a problem that cannot be addressed solely by force or wealth or regulation. Durant concludes that philosophy, values, and the creation of a cohesive culture are essential.

The research and then the writing of the dissertation helped Durant devise and then apply his personal intellectual and philosophical framework of "Perspectivism."

Early on he states that philosophy should be the foundation for politics *qua* political-economic decision-making but notes that it is not. He originated the view later also articulated by E. O. Wilson in *Consilience: The Unity of Knowledge*[7] that philosophy is what *should* be unified with science in order to produce social solutions. (Today Wilson would no doubt say "*sustainable* social solutions.") In other words, the task of philosophy is to help achieve balance between emergent individualism and the larger social construct that requires civic duty and contributions from all if the group is to be secure as well as prosperous. Along with Durant and Wilson, I lament the relegation of philosophy to the "ivory tower" of academia, lost to the public and to the body politic, more pedantry than philosophy.

In his view, philosophy plus history equals wisdom; and politics without either cannot resolve "the social problem" regardless of how much money might be thrown at specific solutions. Durant applies diverse philosophies to his contemporary circumstances to arrive at timeless wisdom, including thoughts about how money creates hoarding and speculation, inheritance incentivizes more of the same, and neither is good for society as a whole.

Wealth creates a leisure class that "buys" knowledge and defines irrational authority, thus destroying the ethical basis of civilization. Durant discussed how a civilization may be characterized by its conception of virtue, which led me to some fruitful exploration of how the United States is a culture that has equated wealth with virtue, leading to a political culture that can be bought because it is based on rule by secrecy, using secrecy to avoid accountability. Today, having abdicated concepts of the good, the beautiful, and the true for a model of primitive accumulation and a materialist set of values, we find that our financial system is what journalist Matt Taibbi called "Griftopia." The financial interests of Wall Street leverage the two-party system as a theatrical sideshow that legitimizes and legalizes massive fraud against the public interest.[8] This is the primary reason why secrecy is necessary for those in power. As I relate in the epilogue, my conversion experience was centered on my discovery that our secret intelligence culture and process is antithetical to democracy, and enabling of plutocracy, neo-fascism, and the total corruption of our government.

Durant defines duty not as unquestioning submission to the group but as individual excellence in thinking and action. Contemporary thinkers such as Ken Wilber and Andrew Harvey (drawing on Sri Aurobindo) have called this integral consciousness, or evolutionary activism.[9] Drawing from Socrates to Spinoza and on, Durant finds that morality is not about freedom of will or individual purpose, but rather about how the group and the individuals as part of the group relate means to ends. I've learned to reframe this today as means (revenue) to ways (policies) to ends (endless war or peace, distributed prosperity or concentrated wealth and broad slavery).

Education

> Knowledge will forever govern ignorance, and a people
> who mean to be their own governors must arm them-
> selves with the power knowledge gives. A popular gov-
> ernment without popular information or the means of
> acquiring it is but a prologue to a farce or a tragedy or
> perhaps both.
>
> —U.S. Founding Father James Madison[10]

The core value of universal education must inform the
most intrinsic function and principle of a democratic society, in order that self-directed reason is inculcated into the
populace. It is only by giving full attention to the task of
universal education that we can reduce our social ills. No
amount of money can have this effect, unless our efforts
are turned away from indoctrinating people into compli-
ance and toward initiating them into being self-governing
and accountable. To this end, Durant draws out the importance of *not* having a standard government-defined education, and of making education fun, exploratory, diverse,
and open-ended. I cannot help but recall here how my
hacker friends consider schools to be prisons.

It is from Spinoza that Durant draws his ultimate vision,
one shared by Thomas Jefferson and James Madison: for
a democracy to be successful, something other than an
anarchist mob, the universal distribution of intelligence,
i.e., wisdom, knowledge, decision-making skills, is essential. Today, with modern networks of communication and
connectivity, the possibility of spreading knowledge and

techniques of reason among the populace is greater than ever before.

For Durant, the mission of philosophy is to facilitate among all people the growth and spread of intelligence, hence also the capacity to use reason to discriminate and make coherent decisions.[11] Unlike history, which reconstructs the past, philosophy seeks to construct a living future. Instead of analysis, synthesis; instead of categorization, reconstruction and redirection. Innovation and creativity come from having a whole-systems perspective, inculcated through education that recognizes a diversity of approaches.

Education and human diversity are the keys to the open-source future of peace and prosperity. There exists a basic mathematics for creating infinite wealth. We start with the fact that the only "infinite" resource we have on Earth is human intelligence. Then we migrate to the fact that today capitalism with all its benefits and flaws is focused on the one billion rich whose aggregate annual income is one trillion dollars a year; *but* they are spending their money foolishly within the industrial-era paradigm that places the power of money in the hands of banks, corporations, and governments, which are corrupt and focused on concentrating old wealth rather than creating new wealth.[12]

My appreciation for the human brain was inspired by James Bamford's discovery[13] that a single human brain is more powerful, using less energy, in a small container, than all the National Security Agency computers combined. Combine this with the insights from C.K. Prahalad's

The Fortune at the Bottom of the Pyramid: Eradicating Poverty through Profits.[14] This author aggregated a tremendous wealth of information in support of his core point: capitalism is focused on the one billion rich whose combined annual income is one trillion dollars a year, while the five billion poor (three billion of them very poor, living on less than two dollars a day) have a combined annual income of four trillion dollars a year.

Now fast-forward to the possibilities inherent in a global population of five billion poor whose annual aggregate income is four trillion dollars—four times that of the one billion rich. Unlike the monetary system of the rich, the monetary system of the poor is rooted in traditional community values, focuses on the sustainable and the practical (conservation not splurging), and inherently believes in the concept of "small is beautiful." The only thing the poor are lacking is access to one another, access to information and education, and access to the power that knowledge and information can give.

No one wants to be poor. In my view, and the view of many authors who have focused on poverty and practical solutions to it, we need to move beyond the industrial-era paradigm of giving them fish, or even the information-era paradigm of teaching them how to fish, and instead move closer to the cosmic paradigm of giving them the tools with which to create their own ingenious means of addressing their problems in their cultural context and their time, while drawing—at their convenience, not ours—on our dispersed knowledge.

This is where the Autonomous Internet can be the liberation technology, not only empowering the poor but leveraging the cognitive surplus[15] of the entire human species.

Transparency

Part of defining and practically applying core values is the achievement of transparency, a.k.a. clarity, in all communications based on these values—clarity with yourself, your loved ones, your neighbors, and with strangers. Through transparency truth can be shared.

Transparency is the new "app" that launches civilization 2.0 as an open-source operating system.[16] Transparency reveals truth (thus leading to accountability), truth engenders trust, and trust is the engine of universal peace and prosperity, the most powerful social currency.

How can "we the people" expand the open-source revolution and leverage Open Source to achieve transparency, eradicate corruption, and restore the public as the sovereign power in our democracy?

This is the heart of my contribution to the open-source everything conversation. I believe that we are entering the third era of the intelligence profession, the decision-support profession. The first era was the era of secret war, spies, and combatants. The second era was that of strategic intelligence as defined by Sherman Kent,[17] but dishonored and dismantled by the growth of the clandestine service and the rise of a military-industrial-intelligence complex able to profit from covert operations regardless of the cost to the ninety-nine percent. This third era, one I have been defining since my Fall 1992 article in *Whole Earth Review*, "E3i: Ethics, Ecology, Evolution, and Intelligence,"[18] is the era of the Smart Nation, of M4IS2, and of the long-envisioned World Brain.[19]

Openness, not secrecy, is the foundation for a healthy community or nation-state. As discussed earlier, industrial-era leadership relies heavily on secrecy, on stove-pipes, on hoarding of information, and generally on a top-down approach that assumes the "leaders" know best and that demands all those "below" them to act "because we said so."

In a closed and secretive system, leaders tend to operate according to ideological bias, and will even prefer to remain uninformed. Basing their decisions on what they want to hear, they will then potentially act in unethical ways that violate the public good. They often prefer to make decisions lacking in reliable intelligence and integrity.

A system of open information exchange based on transparency, where complex problems are treated clearly and directly, allows for all stakeholders to independently consider and evaluate all relevant data—and to share with one another a rich diversity of perspectives. Such a situation creates the conditions for a direct democracy, where an engaged and informed citizenry can determine its own fate through continuous referendum.

Diversity, a Resource of Infinite Wealth

The assumption that underlies my appreciation for diversity is this: the greatest resource we have on Earth is the capacity of the human brain. To answer our existing threats and challenges, we can leave no brain untapped. This includes the five billion poor and especially the three billion most poor, many of them illiterate but possessing enormous innate intelligence and a desire to better themselves that the one billion rich simply cannot conceptualize. Academic specialization is no guarantee of intelligence. The poor possess enormous insight into our world, formed through lives based on survival at the edge. There are also many indigenous cultures around the globe where money is barely used. These cultures retain value systems as well as barter and gift economies that provide necessary tools for redesigning human civilization so it benefits everyone.

At a very simplistic level, "diversity" is accomplished by embracing the inherent value of every brain and the inherent right of every person to "connect" to all others and to information. This particularly includes all those labeled "crazy" by the status quo mind-sets, and it especially includes "truthers" who are penetrating many decades' worth of lies to the public.

I want to repeat a story told to me by Harrison Owen, inventor of Open Space Technology and author of several books, the most recent being *Wave Rider: Leadership for High Performance in a Self-Organizing World*.[20] He was recounting the nature and outcome of a two-day Open

Space Technology conference that he ran for an archi-
tectural and engineering company which had spent more
than two years and a great deal of money—in the millions—designing an airplane whose door would not work
as anticipated. The bottom line: by including everyone
who touched the door, including ground crew, the two-day
conference fixed the problem at a cost to the company of
next to nothing: the costs of the conference. By including all the stakeholders from the bottom up, results were
achieved that could not be achieved by the traditional
"top-down" hierarchical organization.

I have read many other such stories embodying a culture of openness and acceptance for the participation of
all, regardless of rank.

In my view, we must recognize both the value of diversity and the unity that can be achieved by that diversity
when we combine clarity of expression and integrity of
intent. In order to do this, we must learn to share information among what I call "the eight communities of intelligence," each with its own sources and methods, none with
the "whole picture." They are:

1. **Academic.** All those engaged in formalized educational
   activities from Head Start to post-doctoral research.
2. **Civil Society.** All forms of citizen advocacy groups,
   including labor unions and religions.
3. **Commercial.** All forms of business, not only legal, but
   also System D (the informal or underground economy)
   and organized crime.

4. **Government.** All forms of structured government from local to national.

5. **Law Enforcement.** All forms of law enforcement including multinational organizations such as the International Criminal Police Organization (INTERPOL). Does *not* include contractors.

6. **Media.** All media published or purveyed in any form, from bloggers to the "mainstream" media, that are co-opted by the commercial world.

7. **Military.** All forms of military including multinational organizations such as the North Atlantic Treaty Organization (NATO).

8. **Non-Government/Non-Profit.** All forms of non-profit activity registered with a government. Anything not registered falls under Civil Society.

This new meme unifies the knowledge and grassroots experience of the eight communities of intelligence so the human collective becomes the "one body, one mind" implied by the term "noosphere"—a psychic collectivity. We create the World Brain to play the World Game in which we are each a node with an all-access pass to the main event. Each of us can then participate in any and all decisions across all boundaries that we care about, and we create a prosperous world at peace by aggregating our collective intelligence and applying reason and rationality coherently to all analytic, intelligence-gathering, and decision-making processes.

Writing on the Occupy movement, *Rolling Stone* journalist Matt Taibbi proclaimed:

> This is a visceral, impassioned, deep-seated rejection of the entire direction of our society, a refusal to take even one more step forward into the shallow commercial abyss of phoniness, short-term calculation, withered idealism and intellectual bankruptcy that American mass society has become. If there is such a thing as going on strike from one's own culture, this is it.[21]

I share the widespread rejection by the ninety-nine percent of what our political, socio-economic, and ideo-cultural systems have become. A new collective force, a leaderless orchestration, is emergent. If this force can learn to aggregate collective intelligence properly, "we the people" can overcome the ever-more insulated and secretive ruling elite in order to institute a planetary society that works for all.

CHAPTER 5

Integrity, Lies, and Panarchy

Integrity

As a retired Marine Corps infantry officer, I thought I understood the word "integrity," but I have since learned that my understanding was incomplete. Most think of "integrity" in connection with personal character or honor. That is a partial definition of the word, and not the most important meaning in relation to the larger community of humanity and its spiritual as well as physical well-being.

The most important meaning has to do with the quality or condition of being whole or undivided—in a word, completeness.[1] Below are a few reflections of mine posted after attending a meeting where everyone wanted to avoid being specific about the root cause of across-the-board failures of strategy, policy, acquisition, and operations in the Department of Defense—a lack of integrity.[2]

1. Integrity is not just about honor—it is about wholeness of view, completeness of effort, and accuracy or reliability of all elements of the whole.
2. Industrial-era systems do not adapt because they lack integrity and continue to pay for doing the wrong things righter instead of doing the right

thing. The Pentagon is a classic example of such a system.[3]

3. In the twenty-first century, intelligence, design, and integrity comprise the triad that matters most. The truth, the whole truth, and nothing but the truth is the non-negotiable starting position for getting it right, and this is crucially important with respect to the sustainability of the Earth as a home for humanity.

4. Integrity at the top requires clarity, diversity, and balance.

5. Integrity can be compounded or discounted. It is compounded when public understanding demands political accountability and flag officers ultimately understand that they have sworn an oath to uphold the Constitution, not support the chain of command. It is discounted when flag officers are careerists, ascribe to rankism, and generally betray the public interest in favor of personal advancement.

6. Universal access to connectivity and content is a means of accelerating both public access to the truth and the power of the public to offset "rule by secrecy," which inherently lacks integrity at all levels.

In 2008, after first believing in Barack Obama and then recognizing that he was in essence a continuation of the "rule by secrecy" establishment, I wrote a book, *Election*

2008: Lipstick on the Pig.[4] With prefaces from Thom Hartmann and Tom Atlee as well as two others, that book's first chapter discusses what I called "paradigms of failure."

Every major segment of our society—academia, civil society, commerce, government, law enforcement, media, military, and non-government/non-profit—is currently suffering from epidemic lack of integrity, which only gets worse at larger scales of operation, leading to implosion from corruption of intelligence and information-sharing. In *Election 2008* I wrote a section on "legitimate grievances"—on the part of both the U.S. public that has been abused and betrayed by its elected representatives, and the rest of the world where people have suffered unilateral militarism, virtual and actual colonialism, and predatory corporate corruption and looting of every commonwealth on the planet that I know of. Understanding and accepting this sorry state of affairs has been part of my own personal and professional rejection of American exceptionalism and the rule by an elite. This shift in perspective recognizes the need for a new planet-wide consciousness based on open information sharing and direct democracy.

For many years I thought that our elected representatives had been corrupted by corporations and, more recently, by banks (or, I should say, the people who use these structures as veils for their own unethical accumulation of profit). I was in error. As we now know from numerous cases, the most blatant being that of former Congressman Randy Cunningham,[5] it is more often the elected representatives who have been shaking down banks and corporations in order to fund their own ambitions to remain in power and to profit at the expense of the people. Naturally these "little" people found corruption convenient because our larger system—our financial and economic system that is rooted in "money" and allows a monopoly over the creation of money to banks and governments—made it possible for them to leverage their control of the public treasury (a control we all abdicated by failing to be alert and engaged) into personal wealth.

With a tiny handful of exceptions, among whom I count Dennis Kucinich and Ron Paul in the House of Representatives, and Bernie Sanders in the Senate, I consider all of our elected representatives corrupt. In fact, I advocate turning out into the streets all incumbents seeking re-election to a third or later term, if only by refusing to vote for them again. They have betrayed the public trust.

The Executive branch is just as corrupt as the legislators. The Department of Justice has claimed in writing that it has the right to lie to the Court when it deems lying to be necessary.[6] Almost without exception, every Cabinet department and agency is costing the U.S. taxpayer at least twice as much as they merit, since half of that cost is being wasted or otherwise lost to us. From agriculture to health to water, our government is a model of waste, fraud, and abuse.

I want to address the military very briefly as an example of a corrupt system. Four percent of the force (the infantry) takes eighty percent of the casualties, and costs one percent of the military budget.[7] The other ninety-nine percent of the budget goes toward "big systems" that never work as promised and always cost a great deal more and require vastly more logistics support in the field (the joke is, one contractor per laptop). The acquisition system is now so bloated and ignorant it cannot design, order, receive, and test a complete ship or aircraft—worse, there is no strategy for what we really need to support the infantry that only costs one percent of the budget. One estimate is that fully half of the other ninety-nine percent of the budget is fraud, waste, or abuse. Any decision to cut tens of thousands of Army and Marine Corps personnel, while actually increasing the budget for "systems," is a perfect representation of all that is wrong with how we give lip service to the concept of a strong national security force. It is not strong and it is not smart.[8]

The industrial era has been starkly aligned with corruption in all its forms, in large part because those we have trusted with the management of our commonwealth have used secrecy, insider relationships, and a lack of accountability to profit personally. Transparency, truth, and trust—this is the only non-violent alternative to what we have now.[9]

This manifesto is a political and intellectual "call to arms" for carrying out a non-violent revolution that restores the sovereignty of We the People. With Oath Keepers gaining ground among law enforcement professionals, and Ron Paul receiving more support from veterans than all other 2012 Presidential candidates combined, it's possible that the police and military can come together with labor, Occupy, the Tea Party, and Independents to achieve electoral reform and then intelligence, governance, and national security reform.

Lies as Treason

> A man who lies to himself, and believes his own lies, becomes unable to recognize truth, either in himself or in anyone else.
>
> —Fyodor Dostoevsky[10]

Lying is not only unpatriotic, as Ron Paul has said,[11] but lying—any falsification of information—is a corruption of the feedback loop and has consequences within a complex whole-systems environment. Lying is like a cancer—a cancer that is ultimately fatal. If we look at biology, we find that awareness begins at the boundary of the cell, where chemical signals are recognized and either rejected or absorbed into the cell's permeable membrane. If the cell responds to signals that go against the healthy function of the organism, the organism will sicken and die. Similarly, in society we rely on the transmission of accurate and authentic information for the health of the entire social organism. This is why open-source everything is fundamental.

An efficient, innovative, and functional socioeconomic system demands both *intelligence,* defined here as an ability to recognize what information needs to be known to make a sound decision, and *integrity,* an ability to tell the truth and demand the truth. Lies obscure the truth of the work we have to do as individuals and as a society.

Lack of integrity is composed of culturally rooted assumptions about "what works," together with ideological blinders that shut out professional intelligence (decision-support) and instead permit special interests to press their concerns about selling "inputs" rather than being held accountable for "outcomes."[12]

If you lack intelligence and integrity (as do most governments, corporations, and non-governmental organizations including the United Nations), it is virtually impossible to create a prosperous world at peace—a world in which the sciences, the humanities, and faith come together to harmonize human behavior and decisions and thereby produce what are called "win-win" or "nonzero" outcomes.[13]

An authentic relationship to data and intelligence must become the basis for public discourse if the public and its appointed officials are to make sound decisions in the public interest. Any corruption of the process with lies, omissions, or other forms of misinformation is at best a betrayal of the public trust and at worst outright treason.

A major reason why leaders of any organization—not just military organizations—are so easily deceived or mis-served by their own people is because of the "closed" nature of the information delivery system that the CEOs rely on. Absent a completely open and transparent information system, lies and misrepresentations are difficult to identify. They take root and fester, like a cancer within the corporate body.

Thirteen Big Lies

Below are thirteen common lies and their countervailing "possible truths" as put together by Jock Gill, a strategic communicator with a strong sense of ethics.[14] It is not possible to appreciate the importance of transparency, truth, and trust without first understanding the deep roots that these thirteen common lies have grown—*The Open-Source Everything Manifesto* is in large part a primal scream against lies and a plea for integrity as a common good.

LIE 1. The Earth is an open system with infinite supplies and sinks. POSSIBLE TRUTH: Earth is a closed system, and changes that used to take ten thousand years now take three. Humanity is "peaking" the entire system.

LIE 2. Everything must be monetized. POSSIBLE TRUTH: Money is an exchange unit and an information unit. In the absence of holistic analytics and "true cost" transparency, money is actually a toxic means of concentrating wealth and depriving communities of their own resources (e.g., land).

LIE 3. The extreme unregulated free market is the only option for a modern economy. POSSIBLE TRUTH: Information asymmetries and "rule by secrecy" have been clearly documented, proving that the free market is neither free nor fair. A modern economy needs to be transparent, resilient, and hence rooted in the local.

LIE 4. Centralized organization is the only and best option; the network begins in the center and radiates out.

82

POSSIBLE TRUTH: Epoch-A, top-down, hierarchical "leadership" has proven itself to be a failure regardless of its ideology (feudalism, fascism, communism, religious dictatorship). Diversity is the source of agile innovation, and Epoch-B leadership[15] is inherently collective, bottom-up, multicultural, and replete with integrity.

LIE 5. Spectrum (atmospheric frequencies) is a scarce and finite resource best managed by what we knew in the 1920s and '30s. POSSIBLE TRUTH: Open-source everything is "root," and the trifecta for sustainable human evolution is Open Spectrum, Open-Source Software, and Open Data Access.

LIE 6. Houses need furnaces. POSSIBLE TRUTH: Buckminster Fuller, among many others, demonstrated that housing can be created that is self-sufficient in terms of energy, cooling, and heating, and even water catchment and waste disposal.

LIE 7. Power is best generated in remote mega power plants with correspondingly large distribution networks. POSSIBLE TRUTH: *WIRED* magazine outlined how a two-way energy grid that leverages renewable energy across all localities is vastly superior to centralized systems that "bleed" half of the energy while going downstream

LIE 8. Copyright must last longer than a lifetime, and patents must last longer than seventeen years. POSSIBLE TRUTH: Both copyright and patent laws have been manipulated by individuals lacking in integrity. Their efforts to keep useful knowledge from the marketplace have been especially harmful. The Founding Fathers got it right in the first place: Creative Commons copyright and "use it or lose it" patent protocols are best.

LIE 9. The United States of America has nothing to envy in others; we have the best healthcare, the best education, the best broadband, the best lifestyle. POSSIBLE TRUTH: An educated citizenry is a nation's best defense (Thomas Jefferson). The U.S. is now a Third World nation for all practical purposes, with a ten-percent "elite" that has concentrated wealth and a ninety-percent "animal class" that is losing its housing, its health, its clean water, its entire quality of life.

LIE 10. Corporations are people. POSSIBLE TRUTH: Corporations exist on the basis of public charters. Public charters are being granted and managed by government officials who take direction from politicians who have sacrificed their integrity and fail to represent the public interest.

LIE 11. Inconvenient costs and truths may be treated as externalities that do not need to be carried on our "books." POSSIBLE TRUTH: In the absence of an educated citizenry, the public perception of "truth" can be easily manipulated—fog facts, missing information, lost history, manufacturing consent, propaganda, and most recently, weapons of mass deception. There is no counterweight to "power" that wishes to lie.

LIE 12. More of the same old same old will get us new and better results in plenty of time to avoid environmental disruption. POSSIBLE TRUTH: Among intelligent people with integrity, "doing the right thing" instead of doing the wrong thing "righter" is clearly beneficial to all. We can create a prosperous world at peace for a fraction of what we now allow to be spent on war and waste. Pollution is a waste product, an indicator of an inefficient process. Those who persist in defending any status quo are certainly lacking in intelligence (decision-support) and, more often than not, also lacking in integrity.

LIE 13: Tax cuts and trickle-down economics work and create good-paying jobs. POSSIBLE TRUTH: Tax cuts favor the one percent who have already concentrated most of the wealth in the USA, and they invest their gains overseas or in assets that appreciate, not via jobs in the USA.

Lies kill. Lies are a like a road sign that says "Detour" but points over a cliff. Lies prevent the larger public from understanding, evaluating, and responding to any given situation with collective intelligence or wisdom. For example, if the lie "nuclear power is totally safe" is combined with a second "we can trust the government to oversee safety, and the energy company to take all necessary precautions," you get—inevitably—a Chernobyl or a Fukushima.

We live in a culture of lies. Information pathologies such as I reviewed in Chapter 1 have been created over centuries to benefit the few at the expense of the inattentive, distracted, and complacent many. This manifesto is our non-violent articulation of how we can stop being exploited and disadvantaged, and restore the sovereignty of We the People.

We currently have a political culture of epidemic corruption, where facts are distorted to serve the interests of a few,[16] with leaders of both parties, most corporations, and many religions accustomed to deception as a matter of routine.[17] In such a situation, "philosophy" cannot serve its proper function of providing desirable aims and constituting a method based in integrity to fulfill them. In a political culture founded in corruption and deception, it is impossible to achieve balance or stability, and such an inherently unsustainable situation will ultimately collapse.

On the other hand, if one establishes a philosophically grounded culture of clarity, where appreciation for diversity and commitment to integrity are societal norms, one has a promising foundation for progress.

> *Information **costs** money, Intelligence **makes** money.*
> *Intelligence is tailored actionable information.*

All the kum-ba-ya in the world and all the micro-issue think tanks and advocacy groups are ineffective because they lack a strategic analytic model, a process for doing intelligence so as to do informed *activist* democracy, and a call to arms that brings us all together centered on taking back our government or routing completely around it.

Panarchy and Resilience

Complexity demands resilience, and that's what panarchy offers. Resilience in the face of complexity is a challenge even when you apply rigorous intelligence and integrity to develop a coherent and flexible strategy.

On the next few pages I present a few illustrations of panarchy and resilience, followed by several on the "human factor," and finally concluding with some illustrations of the advanced analytic mode of Reflexive Practice—the practice of Buckminster Fuller and Russell Ackoff, and more recently George Soros, Stuart Umpley, and Kent Myers, among others including myself.

We can connect all minds to all information all the time. The "magic" of panarchy is that it combines the wisdom of the crowd, smart mob, here-comes-everybody "cognitive surplus" and "collective intelligence" (two different concepts) with the evolutionary/revolutionary process—the cycle of growth, stasis, break-out, and regeneration with innovation. As an inherently open-source everything system of systems, panarchy exposes fraud, waste, and abuse, eradicates corruption, and in the ideal—at full operational capability—creates infinite wealth in the form of a prosperous world at peace.

The Internet and other advances in telecommunications have made it possible for the public to overcome the information pathologies discussed elsewhere in these pages. This bodes well for humanity.

Two of the best high-level views of panarchy as it pertains to the future of humanity and the Earth are those of Stewart Brand, the arch-father of *Co-Evolution Quarterly*, *Whole Earth Review*, and so many other things, and Venessa Miemis, co-creator with Doug Rushkoff of the Contact Conference,[18] and a wonderful design talent in her own right.

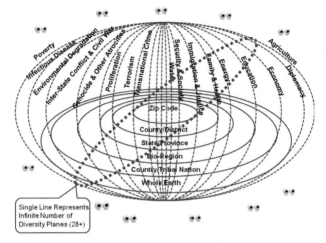

Figure 8: Panarchy Action Model

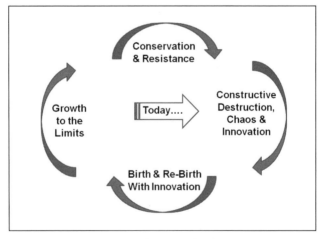

Figure 9: The Panarchy Cycle

Lapse

What is fundamental in Figure 10 is the trumping of governance by culture. When governance breaks down, if the culture is strong, resilience is possible. If the culture is not strong, we have a problem.

The next graphic, Figure 11, a graduate project by Venessa Miemis and accessible via her website Emergent by Design,[19] illuminates how every person who is a participant can (perhaps even must) adopt varying roles suited to their personal inclinations and strengths; and how each of the four main passages in the panarchy cycle benefit from different constellations of public personas.

One more observation: technology is not a substitute for thinking. I have been saying this for decades and

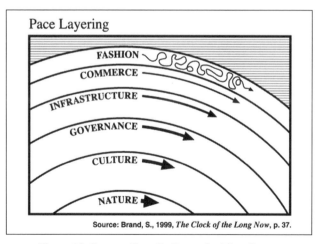

Source: Brand, S., 1999, *The Clock of the Long Now*, p. 37.

Figure 10: Stewart Brand's Panarchy Time Lapse

finally found a graphic (Figure 12) that makes the point crystal-clear.[20]

Panarchy is enabled by information technology, but it is the human mind that actually creates panarchy across all boundaries. The nature of panarchy is a continuous cycle that leverages human intelligence in all its rich diversity. It is urgent that we leverage every possible mind (with a preference for minds that have been liberated and are not inert) through comprehensive full-spectrum integration—in other words, we have to break down all the stove-pipes among academic disciplines, civil society advocacy organizations, commercial entities, government bureaucracies, and so on.[21]

When you do that, resilience is one of the results.

Lies are like sand in the gears of a very complex, delicate machine. Lies steal from the commonwealth. Lies kill. Lies are a cancer on the body of humanity. Integrity is not just the opposite of lies—integrity is the restoration and maintenance of the whole. Integrity is the cosmic mix of transparency, truth, and trust that creates heaven on Earth. Panarchy is heaven; resilience is the Earth and its humanity in a state of balance.

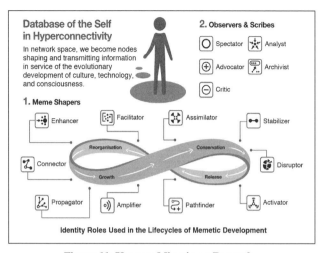

Figure 11: Venessa Miemis on Panarchy

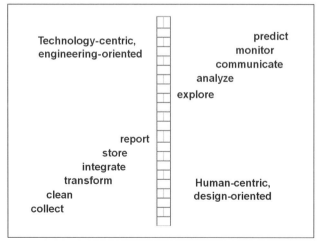

Figure 12: Technology Is Not a Substitute for Thinking

CHAPTER 6

Whole-Systems Thinking

As suggested by the prophecies of indigenous civilizations and elaborated upon by writers such as David Korten, Joanna Macy, and Jeremy Rifkin,[1] we are at the very beginning of an Earth-based awakening to what could be a near-magical integration into a much more intelligent, alive, and nurturing Cosmos than most of us have previously imagined. The process by which this is enacted is what Barbara Marx Hubbard terms "Conscious Evolution" and Tom Atlee calls "Evolutionary Activism."[2]

The evolution of evolution is a transition from unconscious to conscious choice. This is the type of whole-systems thinking championed by the pioneering design scientist Buckminster Fuller and further developed by Russell Ackoff.[3]

The Challenge of Complexity

"World Systems" or the "Whole Earth" is assuredly a complex system of systems, never mind the galaxy and the cosmos! For the Earth alone, we have the geosphere, the hydrosphere, the biosphere (from which some would separate out the anthrosphere or man), and the atmosphere, all in an extraordinary balance necessary to retain oxygen on Earth and provide other conditions for life.

In order for us to live within this finely balanced constellation of complex systems, in order for the Earth to show resilience and last for centuries into the future as an environment for human life, we have to embody three things: a respect for Earth systems and their details in balance; a commitment to discovering and sharing the truth and only the truth at all times about all things; and a commitment to doing no harm.

We have failed on all three counts since abandoning the wiser ways of our indigenous forerunners and falling into the abyss of empire, domination, and separation.[4] I particularly admire the manner in which Thomas Homer-Dixon describes this in *The Ingenuity Gap: Facing the Economic, Environmental, and Other Challenges of an Increasingly Complex and Unpredictable Future.*[5] From that work, which is quite spectacular in acknowledging and integrating the research of others, I draw the following highlights, a tiny handful from the many that can be found in my full online review:

- Dangers increase as man creates complications and misdirects his energy and resources.
- "Hypercapitalism" (a concept credited to David Harvey) compresses time and space, over-produces waste, over-concentrates wealth.
- We know from Chaos Theory that nature will magnify every human perturbation, however miniscule.
- We are deluded in our belief that we can control com-

plexity and predict the outcome of perturbing large systems such as the climate.

- Our social systems are deeply out of synch with nature (less mature), while our economic and technical systems ignore the limits of the natural world.

- Washington, DC, bureaucrats, including senior CIA analysts, do not possess training in the type of whole-systems thought necessary to understand complex realities.

- While the pace of change accelerates, the depth of ignorance and the political resistance to doing the right thing continue to increase as well.

- Delays in policy understanding, decisions, action, and outcomes compound losses over time.

- Humanity has killed one quarter of the planet's diversity to date.

- This systemic imbalance is not sustainable and will soon lead to a devastating collapse without a redirection of human society toward a new relation with the Earth.

- Our ego and our inherited belief structures block us from utilizing our collective intelligence.

- Wealth gaps + migrations = poor global management.

Complex whole systems are almost impossible to address functionally in the absence of intelligence and integrity. An easy way to appreciate the importance of both is provided by Charles Perrow in *Normal Accidents: Living with High-Risk Technologies*,[6] where he discusses three levels of systems, how they fail, and how diagnosis and remediation become increasingly difficult:

1. Simple systems fail in simple ways that are easy to diagnose and correct.
2. Complex systems fail in complex interacting ways that are difficult to diagnose and virtually impossible to remediate from a single fixed point.
3. We are operating within a constellation of complex systems, and the ability to diagnose and remediate is now totally beyond the capacity of any "top-down" entities such as governments or corporations. We have reached our maximum level of incompetence.[7]

This means two things: First, that our industrial-era, top-down, "command and control" systems are not only ineffective, they make problems worse. Second, how we share information and maintain the integrity of the information that we access is vital if we are to be resilient in the face of complex failures and constant challenges.

To the above I add my own observation over decades that many if not most of our technical-support systems are built by the lowest bidder or highest briber (or by the quality-unconscious Chinese), while we fail to practice the precautionary principle (if there is a risk of harm, burden of proof that it is not harmful falls on those proposing the action) in our science and technology, leading to unforeseen hazards and negative feedback loops over time.

Complex Threats to Humanity and the Earth

There are two points of reference helpful for quickly grasping, in a coherent manner, the largest elements of the complex environment that we are disrupting and poisoning.

The first, published in 2003, is a gift to humanity from Jean Francois Richard, at the time Vice President for Europe of the World Bank. He divides our challenges into three groups, listed in the endnote, and they all add up to manmade problems.[8]

The second—and this one with the cachet of having been issued by the United Nations High-Level Panel on Threats, Challenges, and Change—focuses only on high-level threats to humanity, prioritizing ten global threats to our survival—these also are listed in an endnote, and all are man-made problems.[9]

The reality is that all of these threats are created by a system of governance, Epoch-A governance, which relies on top-down, command and control, "rule by secrecy." This structure of governance blatantly lies to the public—and to legislatures, the courts, and international bodies—about the concentration of private wealth. Government for the benefit of corporations externalizes the "true costs" of activities that are detrimental to humanity and the Earth. In the face of systemic deception and self-delusion, all claims to the possibility of sustainable progress are fiction. Tom Wessells makes this point compellingly in his book *The Myth of Progress: Toward a Sustainable Future*,[10] noting that in complex systems, especially complex systems for which we have a very incomplete and imperfect understanding, "control" is a myth, just as "progress" is a myth if you are consuming your seed corn. He demonstrates the flaws of economic theories that are divorced from reality and the "true cost" of goods and services.

No amount of money is going to prevent catastrophe. Absent a commitment to creating a culture of attention and interoperability and information-sharing, we will create our own catastrophes each time we are challenged by what could have been nothing more than a localized disaster.

In *The Collapse of Complex Societies*,[11] Joseph Tainter concludes that if we are to achieve sustainability and resilience, we must nurture at all levels across all boundaries a culture that elevates "problem-solving" as well as the ability to think strategically—an understanding that everything is connected and that getting a grip on the facts of the matter across all boundaries is an essential first step toward conceptualizing workable solutions to complex challenges.

Truth—the combination of intelligence and integrity as well as transparency—is the foundation for both understanding and eradicating these threats, while moving as quickly as possible toward what should be the human mantra toward the Earth and all species, "First, Do No Harm."

Responding with Flexibility

Even with perfect truth there are natural as well as man-made causes that will inevitably present communities with a complex emergency. As predictable as many such emergencies are, what turns disasters into catastrophes is a poor culture of planning and agile response. Conversely, resilience comes rooted in a culture of anticipation, of planning, and of truthful agile responsiveness that empowers all stakeholders, excluding no one. Resilience is the ability to absorb varying forms of shock, attack, disorder, and unanticipated setbacks, and to emerge more or less whole and able not just to carry on but to grow.

David Keys, author of *Catastrophe: An Investigation into the Origins of Modern Civilization*,[12] tells us that natural catastrophes are treated as remote and improbable until they actually occur. Only those civilizations that plan ahead and are well-organized can respond to disasters as they happen, thus reducing the severity of drought, famine, or other challenges. What he does not focus on, covered very ably by Ted Steinberg in *Acts of God: The Unnatural History of Natural Disaster in America*,[13] is how systemic corruption among the elites increases the damage caused by natural disasters, as little flexibility or resilience is built into systems designed to reward the few. People are persuaded or allowed to occupy floodplains and other areas prone to disaster; land speculation runs rampant with local government and insurance company complicity; intermediate measures such as levees are built at public expense. When it all comes crashing down, as with Katrina over New Orleans or the increasingly regular Mississippi River flooding, the rich walk away with their high risks having been amortized, while the poor and minority communities are ruined.

I focus on these negatives in order to emphasize that in combination, a full grasp of the truth—complete transparency for all stakeholders, not just the elite few—and sensible prior planning and community design can eliminate or vastly reduce loss of life and property from man-made or natural catastrophes. There will still be disasters, but they will be readily addressed and quickly remediated. Right now we are doing great harm to the Earth, to our homeland, and to the shared atmosphere. The lies that we continue to tolerate are preventing a sensible response to this mounting crisis.

Resilience begins with a demand for and a commitment to the rigorous application of intelligence that is not restricted or deformed and can take all factors into account. Such a commitment to public intelligence requires an environment of open-source transparency in order to propagate itself.

History

History matters for at least three reasons:

1. It is a baseline for understanding what Stewart Brand and others call "the clock of the long now,"[14] a means of defining time and responsibility in a much longer manner, what our Native American antecedents called "seventh-generation thinking."[15] For example, when we destroy aquifers—sources of pure clean water—by depleting them to the point that they ingest salt water and die for ten thousand years, we are leaving "dry holes" to future

generations. Along with a focus on spiritual and cosmic cycles, we need to be focused, like native peoples, on the practical—leveraging deep knowledge to nurture humanity's sustainability. This means applying the precautionary principle and putting the rights of nature ahead of the rights of exploitation maintained by corporations.

2. History is a baseline against which to measure the present in relation to the future. This is especially important in relation to environmental degradation and demographic setbacks. Understanding history can both reduce hysteria over major changes that are not atypical of the far past, while inspiring greater respect for the need to plan for such changes. If we are going to reconceive and re-engineer society to be resilient and adaptive, we not only have to overcome the fragmentation of knowledge, we must be able to integrate and apply various disciplines of scientific learning in real time. Transparency and truth are essential to this task, trust is the accelerator.

3. A multidisciplinary library of documented lessons from the past, drawn from all cultures, permits new generations to build on the hard-earned experience of our ancestors, minimizing expenditure of blood, treasure, or spirit. Vitality comes from embracing distinct points of view, and in many ways history is a means of achieving appreciation for diversity without feeling confronted. In the same vein, diversity today is a means of tapping centuries of cultural history that would otherwise not be available to an insular culture.

Implicit in each of the above is the expectation that the current generation wants to leverage history, will respect history, and seeks to be responsible in relation to future generations. That is in fact not the case, and therefore "lost history" becomes the norm for many impoverished societies. There exists both a vitality to history when learned and leveraged, and an often significant "opportunity cost" of failing to be responsible about understanding history.

There is no finer explication of these points than *The Lessons of History* by Will and Ariel Durant.[16] Two important points that they bring forward are that morality is strength, and that "the only lasting revolution is in the mind of man." Both of these ideas are central to this manifesto. When a nation-state loses its moral compass, and its domestic and foreign policies are based on lies or insufficient investigation, not only do those policies prove unsuccessful and expensive, they also reduce the legitimacy of the nation-state in the eyes of all others. The era of empire is over for the United States of America—not because the USA has lost its military might but because the rest of the world now has the tools to independently evaluate the truthfulness and coherence of actions, both domestically and internationally. For example, the fact that poverty is on the rise in the U.S. is not lost on other nations.

The second point, that "the only lasting revolution is in the mind of man," is one that our forefathers clearly appreciated. The only lasting revolution is achieved through education, and ideally universal education including women and all minorities. Education is not a privilege, it is a *necessity*. I like to point out that the only inexhaustible resource we have on Earth is the human brain.

We cannot neglect history, yet we persist in doing so, in three ways.

The first is to be oblivious. This has been the case for at least two centuries in the U.S. (much longer elsewhere) with respect to the indigenous knowledge of our forebears, which is particularly relevant to how humans should respect and co-exist with Mother Earth and other species. Other forms of oblivion include government censor (rewriting or concealing facts, often by classifying details as secret—in other words history known to a few but not broadly understood), and also the oblivion regarding critical information about the natural world that is simply not observed or reported.[17]

A second manner of neglecting history is to be arrogant and disdainful of "others." Refusing to consider or respect the history of oppressed peoples, minorities, what some call "lost voices," is to be intellectually and morally impoverished. This is also the case with respect to women and their potential. There is a nuanced feminine instinct for compassion versus the male inclination to focus on black-and-white "justice" as (generally) defined by white males to the detriment of everyone else.[18]

Third is the failure of scholarship, which leaves history chopped up and virtually inaccessible. When combined with the West's disdain for Eastern knowledge and a general reluctance to see the vital urgency of integrating faith and humanities with science, we end up creating "denied areas" where the incomprehension is of our own making.[19] We impoverish ourselves many times over.

Put in another way, it is not possible to divine, discuss, or share the truth of the present without an appreciation for the truth of the past. Not only do we need to delve deeply into the truth of the past, we must extend ourselves to embrace multiple truths from the past—multicultural truths and multi-class truths.[20]

The Fragmentation of Knowledge

Figure 5 in Chapter 1 illustrated the complete fragmentation of knowledge among the scientific and humanities disciplines and sub-disciplines. In Figure 13 I illuminate

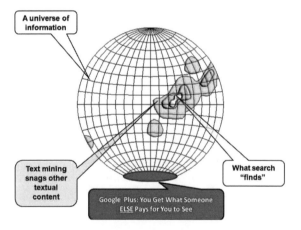

Figure 13: Concept for Achieving a Unity of Knowledge[21]

how the collective intelligence and cognitive science communities might address this fragmentation in the effort to realize a shared goal of creating a World Brain and Global Game.

Even before the digital information explosion, the rapid expansion of scientific, social scientific, and humanities knowledge led to the fragmentation of academic disciplines, and then increasing fragmentation as sub-disciplines developed. Figure 14 depicts how little of the knowledge that exists can be accessed via online search, the default option for all too many people. Add 183 languages in which knowledge is created, and the Babel factor is a multiple order of magnitude worse than a quarter century ago.[22]

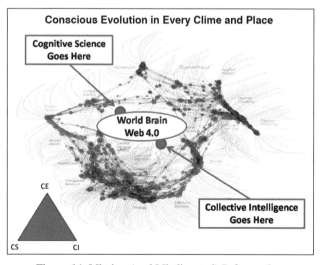

Figure 14: Missing (and Misdirected) Information

There is one other fragmentation that must be addressed. I call them "the eight communities of intelligence" that do not share information with one another in any coherent manner, illustrated in Figure 15. I use a figure, having listed these communities briefly above, because I want to illuminate two points: that they all share a "green" information commons; and that there are outer rings of yellow, orange, and red "restricted" information that demand security and privacy.

Each of these communities has vital original data, information, and analytical insights on any given issue. They are not trained, equipped, organized, nor culturally disposed to share the information they have, not even within their own community.

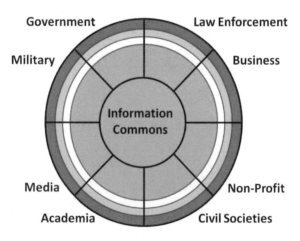

Figure 15: Eight Communities Not Sharing Information

Take poverty, for example, the number-one high-level threat to humanity because the five billion poor create more disease and more environmental degradation than all the corporations combined.[23] Imagine how much more effective we might be if all known information about poverty could be integrated, harvested, distilled, and used to harmonize—voluntarily harmonize through shared data— not just the efforts of all organizations, but the inspired efforts of individuals who could be moved to contribute a specific amount for a specific need for a specific impoverished family.

Or take fresh drinkable water. Each of these communities studies water in a different context, for different purposes, with different outcomes sought. It is virtually

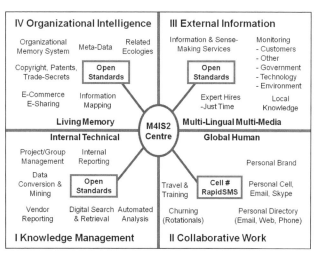

Figure 16: Data in Context

impossible to arrive at a full and honest appreciation of the "true cost" of water for every product, service, or use, because that information is almost impossible to extract even if everyone wanted to.

Each of these communities records their findings and speculations in a different manner. Most importantly, each of these communities fails to record as much as eighty percent of what they know. This is unpublished knowledge that can only be accessed through direct contact and conversation, with the degree of truth that can be exchanged dependent upon transparency and trust in an evolving cycle.

The fragmentation of knowledge is much worse than this. When you look at data in context—what we should be able to do with all information in all languages all the time—we immediately see many more divisions in terms of time, space, discipline, and domain.[24]

	RELIGION IS A SET OF BELIEFS	RELIGION IS A PROCESS
SCIENCE IS A SET OF BELIEFS	Potentially Conflicting	Reinforcing
SCIENCE IS A PROCESS	Conflicting	Potentially Co-Existing

Figure 17: Science versus Religion

Science and Religion

It is helpful at this point to look briefly at both the old relationship between science and religion, which prevented integrity or integral consciousness, and the new relationship favoring unification.[25]

Now contrast that with the visualization in Figure 18, in which science, religion, and philosophy all come together as one.[26]

In the context of humanity on Earth, there can be little doubt that religion and spirituality are forces that likely did not exist until ten thousand years ago yet are now integral parts of the totality of human consciousness; that science is still maturing as a framework for theoretical and applied knowledge of reality; and that philosophy, which has lost much of its appeal to many because of external distractions, remains a vital foundation for addressing the core needs of humanity.

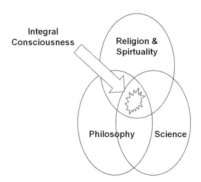

Figure 18: Unification of Religion, Science, and Philosophy

Before I go more deeply into the emergent convergence of science and religion and philosophy—the absolute heart or, in code terms, "root" for operating Spaceship Earth and restoring the consciousness of humanity—I want to focus very briefly on the human mind, heart, and soul (the scientific, the philosophical, and the spiritual), but in an agnostic sense.

Regardless of what religion we each may or may not embrace, regardless of our level of sophistication in science or philosophy, we all share the blessings of being human, of being able to seek, sense, and share.[27]

Transparency and truth, and their multiplicand, trust, are what allow the above human inclinations to yield enormous returns on investment of time and energy. It is the human mind, the human heart, the human soul that are

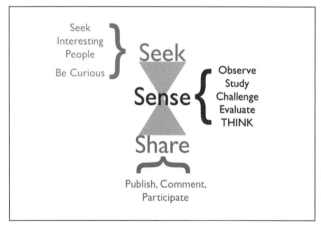

Figure 19: Seek, Sense, and Share

at the root of all that we might call progressive (as well as all that we might call evil). This *Open-Source Everything Manifesto* seeks to shift the power away from the one percent that exploit and diminish the ninety-nine percent, and back to that ninety-nine percent who are capable of creating a world that works for all.

This manifesto concludes with a model for public intelligence in the public interest and a model for informed participatory democracy, within which I will introduce both a strategic analytic model helpful to whole-systems or whole-Earth reflections and a concept for panarchic self-governance in which all citizens have access to the truth—all of the information critical to any subject, translated into any language, available all of the time. It is apparent that truth—the combination of intelligence and integrity as well as transparency—is the foundation for both understanding and eradicating these threats, while moving as quickly as possible in the direction of what should be the human mantra toward the Earth and all species including our own: "First, Do No Harm."

CHAPTER 7

Public Intelligence and the Citizen

Integrity, in my view, starts with the individual human being and grows in a compounded manner from there. The citizen must be an "intelligence minuteman."[1]

The next step in our exploration, beyond the individual human mind and soul, can be found in mass collaboration and particularly in collective intelligence. Many book titles have sought to describe the underlying foundation—not only those associated with collective intelligence as I discussed in Chapter 1, but also the literature on cultural, economic, and sociological "tipping points,"[2] as well as the literature on the "power of the powerless" as a "a power government cannot suppress."[3]

My point is this: the achievement of panarchy is in my view inevitable. The only questions are "how soon?" and "can we avoid violence?" Alvin Toffler nailed this in his book *Powershift: Knowledge, Wealth, and Violence at the Edge of the 21st Century*[4] when he stated that information (I would say intelligence or decision-support, i.e., information tailored to support a decision) is a substitute for wealth and violence, time and space. That is precisely the focus of this book: everything is information, information is everything, and if we open-source everything we are really opening up all information and all minds to creating the equivalent of heaven on Earth—that is to say, a world that works for all in which no "bug," i.e., no corrupt act, no lie, no betrayal of the public trust, can escape notice in near-real time.

Taking Control of the Future

We find ourselves in a tumultuous environment, where every day is a challenge. The threats are beyond the understanding of any one person or organization or country, and intelligence and the rule of law are too often subverted to serve the interests of a tiny elite. This chaotic and corrupt political culture is mirrored by a system of noetics (a consciousness culture that is unconscious, with controlled opposition and theatrics eliminating deliberative dialog and participatory democracy) that blocks the individual attaining clarity and self-knowledge. In contemporary society, the nature of man's relationship to himself, his community, to science and spirit is at best poorly understood, at worst manipulated and subverted.

In this chapter I:

- provide a high-level view of how to achieve public intelligence in the public interest.
- present an immediately implementable model for integrating citizen participation, public intelligence dissemination, and political dialog and deliberation into one seamless online system as an umbrella for an infinite range of Town Hall meetings.

- address how a World Brain and Global Game can create the noosphere imagined by Pierre Teilhard de Chardin and amplified in José Argüelles' *Manifesto for the Noosphere*.[5]

We are at a tipping point for restoring the intelligence and integrity of the Republic. Time is the one strategic variable that cannot be replaced nor purchased. I believe that all the consciousness and good intention in the world will be irrelevant if we cannot arm the public with intelligence (decision-support) on all topics at all levels of governance.

Our first challenge is to redirect "intelligence" away from secret obsession and toward open-source realities. I illustrate this in Figure 20.

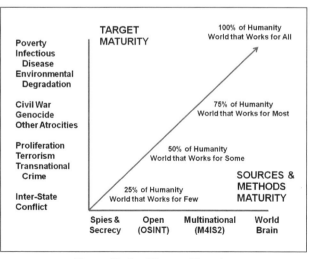

Figure 20: Intelligence Maturity

Many readers will recognize the goal—to create a world that works for all, for one hundred percent of humanity—as one articulated by Buckminster Fuller. One can immediately see that an obsession on inter-state conflicts, most of which have been started or electively joined by the U.S. government acting "in our name" (and generally *without* the Constitutionally required approval of Congress), and an equivalent obsession with secret sources and methods are depicted as the most immature state.

Our second challenge is to end the reliance on elites and experts and demand complete transparency of all decisions at four levels of decision-making (strategic, operational, tactical, and technical). Our collective judgment

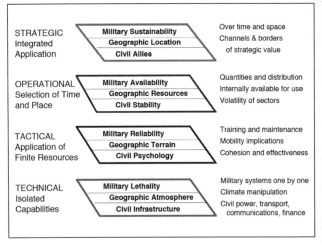

STRATEGIC Integrated Application	Military Sustainability Geographic Location Civil Allies	Over time and space Channels & borders of strategic value
OPERATIONAL Selection of Time and Place	Military Availability Geographic Resources Civil Stability	Quantities and distribution Internally available for use Volatility of sectors
TACTICAL Application of Finite Resources	Military Reliability Geographic Terrain Civil Psychology	Training and maintenance Mobility implications Cohesion and effectiveness
TECHNICAL Isolated Capabilities	Military Lethality Geographic Atmosphere Civil Infrastructure	Military systems one by one Climate manipulation Civil power, transport, communications, finance

**Figure 21: Four Levels of Analysis
for Decision-Support**

and say-so must be reasserted if we are to balance our budget and achieve normal sustainability and resilience in the face of unanticipated disasters.

This is the beginning of constructing an "analytic model" through which citizens can demand their full engagement. In addition to the four levels, we have the three closely entwined slices: civil, natural-geographic, and military (or any other field such as energy or health). Furthermore, any decision made in isolation (e.g., a strategic military decision), without regard to the implications across the other levels and slices, is bound to be a costly and regrettable decision—the elective invasions of Afghanistan and Iraq stand out as recent examples.

The U.S. government has been controlled by a two-party tyranny that has always been corrupt, but this corruption went nuclear in the 1980s when both parties conspired to start borrowing one trillion dollars a year—one third of the federal budget—so as to keep on handing out taxpayer funds (or taxpayer obligations for borrowed funds) to the special interests funding their perpetual grip on power to the exclusion of Independents and the other four accredited but excluded active national political parties (Constitution, Green, Libertarian, Reform).

In Figure 22 I illustrate the integrated analytic model that was created by the Earth Intelligence Network, combining the top-ten high-level threats to humanity as prioritized by the UN's High-Level Panel on Threats, Challenges, and Change in 2004, and our own work examining Presidential transitions over a quarter-century to identify the twelve core policies that must be harmonized if we are to be coherent (effective) as a Republic.

Note that fifty percent or more of our national resources are being wasted for lack of both intelligence (sound decision-making based on facts instead of ideology) and integrity (massive corruption across all three branches of the federal government—Congress, the Executive, and most recently the Supreme Court). For this short manifesto, I will only comment generally, with examples centered in three areas:

1. Corruption. The standard "rate" within Congress for an earmark is five percent. This means that a specific Senator or Representative will ensure the inclusion in the

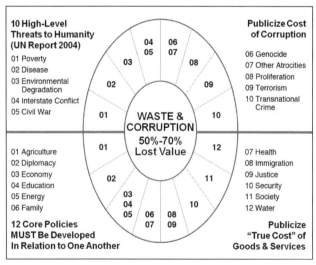

Figure 22: Holistic Analytics as Antidote to Corruption

national budget of anything that is asked—however insane or unnecessary it might be—as long as they can count on receiving five percent of the total awarded as a contribution to their Political Action Campaign (PAC).

2. Analytic Ignorance. The sad reality is that the U.S. government does not make decisions based on intelligence (decision-support) but rather based on corruption and ideology. The decisions to go to war in Afghanistan and Iraq that have cost us lives and trillions of dollars, as well as the decisions to deregulate the financial industry, were corrupt and ideological decisions made in refusal of all the evidence to the contrary.[6]

3. True-Cost Ignorance. Despite decades of irrefutable work by a broad combination of academics, civil society activists, corporate whistle-blowers, government employees, investigative journalists, and non-governmental researchers, governments and corporations generally (not just in the U.S.) all refuse to integrate into their decision-making process the total true cost of any good, service, or behavior. Water, child labor, tax avoidance, and extreme pollution are all examples of externalized costs that should be—but are not—integrated into every calculation.

Calculating True Costs

Given the refusal by both governments and corporations to be responsible about calculating true costs of each good and service, it's no wonder that virtually every government policy, acquisition, and operations decision is uninformed—at the same time that the public is uninformed for lack of public intelligence. . . . Hence special-interest lobbying is uncontested.

It was this realization, learned from Dr. Herman Daly, the pioneer of "ecological economics,"[8] that led me to the fact that government is not "doing" intelligence and therefore the government is not perceiving the truths—the true costs, the true options—that need to be perceived in the public interest.

The "new craft of intelligence" that I began developing in 1988 and first published a book on in 2002[9] restores the integrity of the entire intelligence process (from requirements to collection and processing to analysis). Figure 24 illustrates what should be the four quadrants of the new craft of intelligence within any nation-state. Perhaps

---

True Cost of One White Cotton T-Shirt
Non-Organic, Foreign-Made, 200g/7oz

- Water: 570 gallons (45% irrigation)
- Energy: 8 kWh (machines), 11 to 29 gallons fuel
- Travel: 5,500 to 9,400+ miles
- Emissions: NO_x, SO_2, CO, CO_2, N_2O, volatile compounds
- Toxins: 1-3g pesticides, diesel exhaust, heavy metals (dyes)
- Child Labor: 17 countries, 50 cents/day
- Buy Online: http://true-cost.re-configure.org

Figure 23: Example of a True-Cost Calculation[7]

more importantly, but not so tangibly illustrated, is the fact that no single nation-state can do this. I used to say that you could not have a Smart Nation without a smart engaged citizenry, and that still applies, but now I emphasize that a Smart Nation cannot exist without being part of a very transparent and truthful multinational network of information-sharing and sense-making that creates trust and enables true cost to be deeply and consistently understood.

It is vital to create this new capability. For twenty years I have labored in advocacy for creating an Open-Source Agency that would be the national proponent for all things open, but particularly F/OSS, OSINT, Open Data Access, and Open Spectrum. That is how we create a Smart Nation.[10]

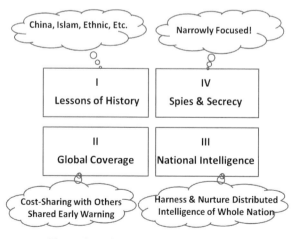

Figure 24: The New Craft of Intelligence

I want to provide two more illustrations of how we must as a public be able to think holistically and understand that the way government and business are now organized, with the banks completely out of control, is catastrophic. Health is an area where we can make immediate corrections, using information in the public interest. The best reference I have discovered is "The Price of Excess: Identifying Waste in Healthcare Spending,"[11] which finds that half of every healthcare dollar is waste. Now combine that with a refusal on the part of politicians and policymakers to be responsible about holding individuals accountable for healthy lifestyles and organizations accountable for healthy environments, while also permitting the Medical-Industrial Complex to repress information on natural and alternative cures, and you find that the fifty-percent waste is against the high-cost medical part of the holistic solution, while the opportunity cost outside of that is seventy-five percent of the total solution. I illustrate this in Figure 25.

Apart from being patient-centered, which the health industry is not, this diagram is important in illustrating both the power of information and the three areas where we are not focusing our efforts to achieve massive savings: healthy lifestyles, healthy environments free of toxins (instead, we ignorantly permit the poisoning of our food and air and water), and natural or alternative remediation including Chinese and Indian (Ayurvedic) Traditional Medicine. We have already established that the fourth area, surgical and pharmaceutical remediation, is fifty percent waste.

Medicare is on everyone's mind these days. My understanding is that the unfunded deficits in the Medicare out-years can be made to disappear if we simply acquire an honest government that does not legislate special deals and prohibit negotiation. My understanding is that the top seventy-five drugs bought under Medicare today at the "asking" price that we are not allowed to negotiate can be purchased for one percent of that cost by using legal wholesale channels from Thailand to South Africa to Turkey. This is consistent with the known "fee" that members of Congress charge for delivering earmarks: five percent of the cost of the taxpayer-funded project. In other words, Congress mandated that we pay one hundred percent of the asked cost instead of one percent of that, the true cost, because

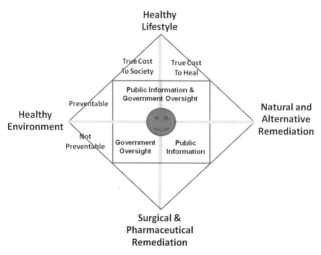

Figure 25: Health Analytics, 360 Degrees

it secured their five percent. They are discounting and distributing the public treasury for no better reason than to claim their "cut" of an inherently corrupt transaction.

Health is not just about humans, and healthcare is not an "entitlement" as much as it is a responsibility. We need to create a global grid for health that encompasses every human, every animal, every form of vegetation, every form of organization, every type of activity. This would be a grid that creates an information "cocoon" within which every person can be intelligent about their health in all respects—if they have integrity, they are healthy. If they do not, they die sooner than they might have otherwise.[12]

The wanton poisoning of the air, food, and water by industries that have obtained exemptions from all manner of precautionary measures is a particularly dangerous fraud, one that citizens should be studying with care, and then disseminating the findings. There is no question that our food is poisoned, and that many household products are dangerous to the health of our children. Combine this with the "Pandora's Poison" of an industry based on chlorine and plastics, and you have a recipe for self-destruction.[13]

Water is the "next big thing" and the fastest way to demonstrate the value of public intelligence in the public interest. Decisions have been made over the past half-century that are easily seen now in retrospect to have been against the public interest. We are on the verge of making other decisions (e.g., Keystone) and allowing practices such as fracking that are totally against the public interest if the facts can be marshaled in a compelling public manner. If they can be ignored, they will be.

What we do every day to the little fresh water that remains is a crime. The aquifers are sinking fast, in part because we allow Coca-Cola, Nestlé, and others to pay nothing for groundwater that they then poison and sell in plastic bottles that each required more fresh water to make than is contained in the bottle itself. When an aquifer empties, if there is a path to seawater, that seawater rushes in to fill it, and it will be ten thousand years, if at all, before that aquifer is again filled by fresh water.

Figure 27 emphasizes that the greatest value in the intelligence domain—and the least expensive option—lies in

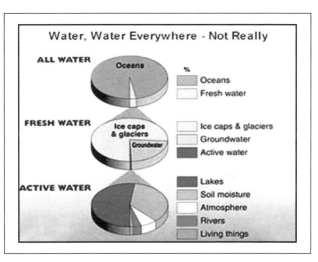

**Figure 26: Fresh Active Water in Larger
Water-Reality Context**

the bottom half where sharing is the core value. Meanwhile the upper half, if shared, would yield much greater value for one hundred percent of humanity. This is what government should be doing in our name but is not. The U.S. federal government, like most governments, is a collection of "stove-pipes," organized by Cabinet departments and by agencies, each of which works diligently to optimize its "budget share" in relation to all others. Information is not shared, and no one does strategic intelligence (decision-support). The Office of Management and Budget, where the "Management" was never strong and was completely discarded in the 1970s, would be one place where such a function could be placed.

The bottom line is that our government is not intelligent about how it pursues the public interest, because

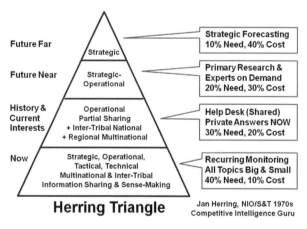

Figure 27: Herring Triangle of Need versus Cost

its decisions are not informed decisions (and its interest is generally not the public's).

Doing Public Intelligence

I have long emphasized the importance of bloggers as citizen "intelligence minutemen" and described how individual citizens could affix themselves like leeches to specific locations, products, companies, or personalities. Think of this as a form of distributed investigative journalism where the most important attributes are a) a personal commitment to the public good; and b) eyes on the target, i.e., co-location with whatever is being monitored. That is in the collection arena. In the analytic arena, again millions of citizens can be distributed but they also can be collaborative, sharing information and coming together to make sense. What has been lacking is an all-inclusive model for achieving that objective.

Figure 28 is an illustration of Citizen Monitors everywhere, implementing an Open-Source Everything approach to public policy and public spending.

Citizens can come together to be better informed than any one of the eight communities acting alone, and citizens can dominate a holistic policy process by using a strategic analytic model that sees everything in relation rather than in isolation. This needs emphasis, and this is why the Occupy movement is so important: we need a massive cultural change that engages every citizen in a constant global endeavor to understand, to make sense, to decide, as a collective, for the good of all. In other words, we must create the noosphere.

It is an old saying in the intelligence world that novices argue about data, journeymen discuss models, and masters talk about assumptions. For this manifesto, I have touched on data (we have to get a "true cost" data) and now will provide a model for how to organize citizen intelligence. The assumptions will be touched on in the final portion of this chapter when I discuss creating the World Brain and Global Game.

The model is visible in Figure 22 above, "Holistic Analytics," and Figure 29 provides what may be an easier-to-grasp, three-dimensional matrix that brings together in one place the top ten threats to humanity, the twelve core

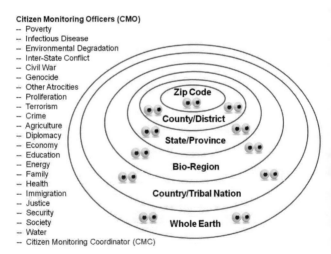

Citizen Monitoring Officers (CMO)
-- Poverty
-- Infectious Disease
-- Environmental Degradation
-- Inter-State Conflict
-- Civil War
-- Genocide
-- Other Atrocities
-- Proliferation
-- Terrorism
-- Crime
-- Agriculture
-- Diplomacy
-- Economy
-- Education
-- Energy
-- Family
-- Health
-- Immigration
-- Justice
-- Security
-- Society
-- Water
-- Citizen Monitoring Coordinator (CMC)

Zip Code
County/District
State/Province
Bio-Region
Country/Tribal Nation
Whole Earth

Figure 28: Citizen Monitors Everywhere

policies that must be harmonized, and the eight demographic players that will define the future regardless of what we do unless we rise to the challenge of creating first a Smart Nation and then a global noosphere. Governments and corporations will not do this for us—the *last* thing they want is an educated citizenry that is attentive and insistent on intelligence and integrity in all domains.

This Citizens Analytic Model is four-dimensional in nature. It focuses on the ten high-level threats to humanity in prioritized order, ensures that each threat is addressed by all policies harmonized among themselves, respects the imperative of creating solutions that will be acceptable to the eight demographics that will "own" the future, and adds value by respecting and integrating what can

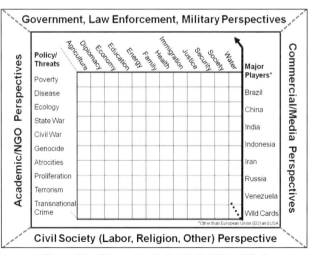

Figure 29: Citizens Analytic Model Simplified

be known—the informed but diverse perspectives—from and by the eight communities of intelligence: academic, civil society including labor and religions, commercial, government, law enforcement, media, military, and non-governmental/non-profit.

What has been lacking to date in the open world has been a strategic analytic model that allows shared information to leave no fraud, waste, or abuse (corruption) unnoticed, and to harmonize a diversity of endeavors without imposing "control." Although open data access is vitally important, an open analytic model is equally vital to accelerate information-sharing and sense-making.

Blogging for Public Intelligence

The Linux model is the model for public intelligence—a globally distributed network of volunteers whose reputation is developed over time in a very transparent manner, all operating in a voluntary hierarchy that provides coherence and quality control.

Imagine if each zip code organized itself in relation to each of the ten high-level threats to humanity, with a matrix-like counterpart organization of bloggers following each of the twelve core policies (and all other policies of interest at that level) such that on a daily basis the collective has the pulse of its sovereign terrain, while also, on a continuing basis, carrying out special studies of specific companies, individuals, or patterns of behavior considered to be detrimental to the common good.

Imagine if each zip code organized itself in relation to each of the budget-line items in the county, state, and national budgets, ensuring a public oversight function over how and when money is or is not spent.

This is a level of scrutiny that does not exist today. Despite many excellent efforts, generally organized at a national level, no one has devised or put into place a "web" of information-sharing and sense-making that is able to leap across all boundaries: locational, technical, ideo-cultural. Participatory democracy without public intelligence is a charade.

At *Phi Beta Iota the Public Intelligence Blog,* a wealth of free information is available, including online handbooks about how to "do" public intelligence in the public interest.

Participatory Democracy

Now I turn to how an informed public can become an engaged public, with the power that knowledge gives, restoring the Republic and serving as an example for the rest of the world.

Today the political "dialog" is a false one—theatrical, rhetorical, and driven by ideology not intelligence. The politicians are prone to lying, their primary objectives are re-election and personal enrichment, and this in turn allowed Wall Street and the various industrial-era complexes (agriculture, education, energy, justice, military) to dismantle regulatory oversight and feed a frenzy of greed by the top one percent at the expense of everyone else.

Figure 30 is a diagram that illustrates how I would organize a free online deliberative dialog system that connects all citizens to all information—including true-cost information—and is capable of framing deliberative dialog in relation to reality and to trade-offs, both ignored by the two-party tyranny in the U.S. and their counterparts across most of the world.

To be effective, an informed participatory democracy must have several capabilities:

- The capability to learn and be informed on anything, and within that capability, an understanding of true costs over the life of each and every system, product, or service—socio-ecological economics.

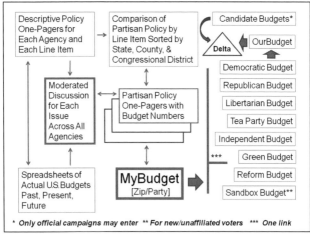

* *Only official campaigns may enter* ** *For new/unaffiliated voters* *** *One link*

Figure 30: Participatory Democracy Online

- The ability to aggregate informed views so as to illuminate alternative trade-offs within a consensus framework that strives to achieve a balanced and therefore sustainable budget.
- The ability to oversee all legislation and all executive decisions at all levels (local to global) and weigh in on the policy process as it is developing, not after the fact.
- The ability to monitor implementations and outcomes, holding executives and legislators accountable for their decisions.
- The ability to intervene to reverse an implementation or outcome that is going badly, or to recall an executive or legislator who is failing to pursue the public interest as defined by the public.

All the above translate into a functional requirements document that I have placed online[14] and will not repeat in detail here. The highlights:

- Everyone gets to play themselves, anonymously or in true name. What this means is that you get to decide your level of participation, and if you choose to be part of the decision-making collective on any given issue or at any given location, you have that right and have access to both the information and tools necessary to carry out deliberative dialog.
- The only visible identifiers are zip code and political preference. This is essential in order to aggregate concerns, preferences, and views by location, political grouping, and of course issue.

- After aggregation by political preference, the larger groups are shown true costs of any options they propose, and a deliberative dialog process takes place at a macro level (a limited number of aggregated voice composites instead of everyone speaking at once).

- All of this takes place in the context of constantly visible real and alternative budgets including a balanced budget, and a constantly visible near-real-time Earth Dashboard. An Earth Dashboard, something Medard Gabel has been developing,[15] integrates the power of what can be known in near-real time across all domains, and the power of advanced visualization such as Robert Horn and Peter Morville have pioneered.[16]

- Candidates are expected to provide clear policy objectives with their budget assumptions, for comparison with both existing partisan and the "consensus" budgets created online.

- Not depicted here, but easily achievable, are coalition budgets that select some policy solutions from one candidate, others from another candidate.

- Eventually candidates will be required to declare their cabinet in advance, and to provide a balanced budget across all policy domains, ideally crowd-sourced, before election day.

In Figure 30, "Delta" stands for difference—we are now at a point where informed, engaged citizens can both create their own common-sense policies and budget while demanding that candidates demonstrate they can do the same. This means full transparency: an end of rhetoric and a restoration of integrity to our electoral system so long corrupted by the two-party tyranny and their Wall Street masters.

Before we can achieve the above "Nirvana" of authentic democracy, there are two missing elements: first, close to half of the eligible voters do not vote; and second, there is no source of trusted "true cost" information for each citizen. Just as the elective war on Iraq was sold as a war that would pay for itself, where we would be welcomed as liberators, it now turns out that 935 lies were told (all documented by truth.dig) and the war has cost us more than three trillion dollars and thousands of deaths.

This lack of accurate, trustworthy information about the true cost of any given policy, product, service, or behavior is paralyzing all action. The U.S. specifically, but most of the rest of the world as well, is coming off a half century in which each of the eight communities has been a party to what I call the "Paradigms of Failure."[17]

It merits mention that I have provided all this information to Americans Elect, a brilliant idea badly executed behind closed doors, and they have refused to change their Epoch-A mindset of "we'll decide who qualifies, we'll retain the ability to cook the books." An Epoch-B mindset would provide the public with the tools to do the job and get out of the way, focusing efforts on ensuring the integrity of the whole.

Creating the World Brain and Global Game

There is absolutely no question in my own mind that we can in the very near term create a Smart Nation here at home, and a prosperous world at peace that restores the harmony and sustainability of the commons writ large. A cosmic truth and reconciliation movement is in the making, and it starts with us.

"We are the ones we have been waiting for" is a very powerful meme that has been diluted by selfishness—even the best-intentioned endeavors have chosen to be little stove-pipes, disconnected from all others. We can harmonize and accelerate our goodness with information. Truth is free. Intelligence is free. Integrity is free.

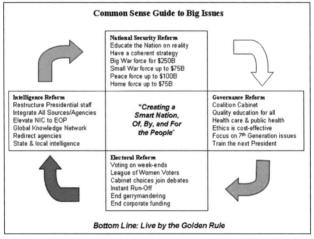

Figure 31: Four Reforms Toward a Smart Nation

There is nothing wrong with the United States—or the world at large—that cannot be stabilized and reconstructed by restoring the intelligence and integrity of all our organizations across the eight communities (academic, civil society, commerce, government, law enforcement, media, military, non-governmental/non-profit). To do that, We the People must first restore our own intelligence and integrity, then reach out to others all over the world to create the World Brain and Global Game—what the technocrati might think of as Web 4.0, and what members of the consciousness community call noosphere.

Figure 31 is my depiction of the four reforms we need to effect in the USA to become a Smart Nation able to nurture the rest of the world to our own common good as our model is adopted.[18]

It is not enough to save ourselves, although putting a stop to unilateral militarism, virtual colonialism, and predatory immoral capitalism is certainly a very good start. We must also help others leverage information to achieve infinite wealth using shared information and multinational decision-support. Figure 32 offers some areas of possibility.

It is vital to pursue initiatives such as the Open Farm endeavor to create open-source tools (hardware) that are low-cost, easily replicable, and easily repaired as well as energy-smart.

Barry Carter nailed it in the 1990s in his book *Infinite Wealth: A New World of Collaboration and Abundance*[19] with his emphasis on the need to deconstruct bureaucracies and liberate individuals to self-organize. We still have not come together to recognize that the fastest way to create infinite stabilizing wealth on Earth for all is to offer the three billion poor free cell phones and free access to information—not necessarily the Internet via smart telephones, but rather dumb phones with free access to call centers that can answer any question on demand by leveraging the Internet and back-office processing.

I am conceptualizing here the concept of free access to substantive information being a human right or privilege, however you might wish to define it, but being an absolute non-negotiable attribute for any nation or community that wishes to be resilient and to prosper in a sustainable fashion.

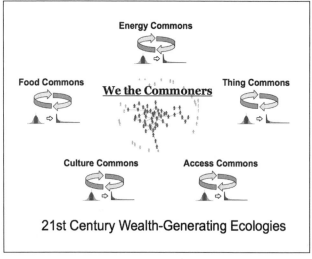

Figure 32: Liberation Technology Domains

I see cities, countries, nations, regions recognizing that the relatively minor cost of a call center is well worth its benefits—capable in all necessary languages and able to handle the load of calls with a mix of centralized and distributed participants, some paid, most volunteers. This then becomes the lever that will move the community or nation out of poverty and into a position where the distributed intelligence of the community or nation is able to create infinite wealth while also achieving a sustainable peace.

Such a network of call centers will only be valuable and achieve its ends if every person on the planet has a personal cell phone, particularly the poorest of the poor. The cell phone serves as a home address for the indigent, a personal wallet for the impoverished, a memory for the illiterate. Liberation technologies can make free cell phones and free access to the airwaves real now.

India is the most complex testing ground for this idea, and one hopes they will consider its adoption.

Lastly, in my final graphic I wish to share a deliberate strategy for creating a prosperous world at peace.[20]

The essence of this manifesto is found in the proven fact that transparency and truth foster trust, and trust lowers the cost of doing business. The industrial era carried the information pathologies to extremes and enabled corruption at the highest levels, using secrecy to avoid accountability. The above strategy starts with reality truthfully described and shared, builds up through applying open-source everything with integrity such that multinational information-sharing and sense-making—and the integration of all faiths and all values—are possible. The strategy ends with total accountability, one for all and all for one, along with the Golden Rule and Love Not War. Gandhi, Martin Luther King, Jr., and Ron Paul all have it right. We have failed as an economy and as a society because we lost sight of both the irreplaceable value of the human with dignity, and of the truth. As I say, the truth at any cost lowers all other costs.

Each of us has both intelligence and integrity in full measure. We have allowed the "empire of illusion and the triumph of spectacle"[21] to subordinate our intelligence and integrity. Now is the time to rise up, non-violently, with intelligence and integrity, to restore America the Beautiful and to then empower the three billion poorest with free access

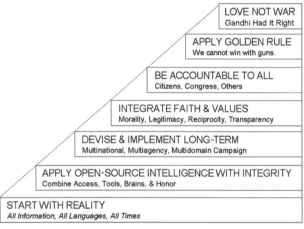

**Figure 33: From Truth to a Prosperous
World at Peace**

to the Internet and cybersphere, and eventually the psychic collectivity of the noosphere. In that context, we ensure the integrity of the information (both for the domain under consideration, e.g., agriculture, and for the whole, e.g., including family, food, health, immigration, and water). We also ensure the integrity of the connection between reality and all budgets both current and being planned for the future. "Control Fraud" is a term new to me, referring to the criminal neglect of legislatively mandated duties by the executive of any given government.[22] I do not fault Wall Street for its high crimes—they were enabled by a corrupt federal government, a government where specific individuals in elected, appointed, and civil service or uniformed positions have betrayed the public trust repeatedly. Without integrity, a government lacks both efficacy and legitimacy. My personal goal is the restoration of both for the Republic, at the federal, state, and local levels, non-violently, as quickly as possible.

We can create heaven on Earth. It is in the context of a non-violent culture committed to appreciative inquiry and informed engaged citizenship that a nonzero (win-win) society can be achieved, crossing all borders, embracing all communities.

Conclusion

I am personally optimistic. I share the widespread view that we are entering a new epoch during which we can achieve conscious evolution and the elevation of humanity to a constructive steward of the Earth.

We must heal ourselves first, branching from those of us able to afford access to the Internet and the luxury of time in which to be both reflective and activist. Then come the five billion poor and especially the three billion extreme poor, whose human brains are the one inexhaustible resource we have. It could reasonably take no less than a quarter century and perhaps as much as a century to achieve the maturation of *Homo sapiens*.

I can only speculate, but I am fairly certain that the noosphere is not limited to human minds but includes the minds of all living things.

Jeff Bezos, founder of Amazon.com and all-around innovator, has said that we are at the very beginning of a massive, virtually unimaginable "break-out" for humanity, to which I would add, "and for all forms of life as well."[23]

Empowered by open software, hardware, spectrum, data access, and intelligence, we are within reach of open democracy.

We must destroy the two-party plutocracy system that has been funded by Wall Street and allowed the one percent to concentrate most of the wealth in their hands, not only in the USA but around the world. I favor Truth and Reconciliation, not vigilante violence. The one percent has to *want* to labor with us to create a world that works for all. Only public intelligence in the public interest can create such a compelling force for the common good as to succeed in the face of heretofore entrenched and powerful opposition and dominance.

Connected, we are One.

My Conversion Experience

I have a somewhat unique perspective on this time of trans-formation. A quarter-century ago, in 1988, I morphed from being a spy and secret intelligence professional into being a champion for public intelligence in the public inter-est. When I say "public intelligence," I refer to decision-support that is open: ethical sources, ethical methods, ethical objectives. Decision-support (or intelligence) is not information; it is not even specialized information such as operating manuals, finance newsletters, or anything that is broadcast or used by more than one person.

Decision-support (intelligence) is information that has been deliberately collected, processed, analyzed, and pre-sented in response to a specific intelligence requirement from a specific person or decision-making organization. Without the requirement, it should not be done and has no value. Public intelligence thus refers to doing for the public—using only legal and ethical sources and methods. This is what the $80-billion-a-year U.S. secret intelligence community does—very badly—for only one person, the President of the United States of America.[1]

Here is how my metamorphosis happened:

At the age of thirty-six, it was my privilege in 1988 to be invited by the leadership of the Marine Corps Intelligence

Division[2] to help create the Marine Corps Intelligence Center, at the time the newest intelligence capability in the United States. Because it was the newest facility, I was able to take a "clean sheet" approach to the challenge, resulting in a situation where the analysts had better desktop workstations and a better culture than elsewhere in the secret world, at that time an archipelago of disconnected capabilities.

I came to the position with decades of overseas experience as the son of an oil engineer, as an infantry officer, and as a clandestine case officer (spy) for the Central Intelligence Agency (CIA). I was a Reagan Republican, believing in the importance of the U.S. government and the USA as forces for good. It never occurred to me to question policies that were being devised "in my name," such as trickle-down economics (a false flag for what is really concentration of wealth) or the continued commitment to U.S. global hegemony and support to forty-two of the forty-four dictators on the planet.[3] I never stopped to consider the deeper implications of how the secret world did what it did, why the secret world did what it did, or the effect of the secret world—and its military-industrial "big brother"—on humanity.

As the senior civilian, both the Special Assistant and the Deputy to Colonel Walter Breede, III, USMC, I was responsible for a $20-million budget to create a state-of-the-art covert intelligence facility with access to all secret messages summarizing intercepted telephone calls and other forms of communication (from the National Security Agency), to imagery of military and other "high-priority" targets (from the National Reconnaissance Office), to messages

144

offering reporting from clandestine Human Intelligence (HUMINT), the latter from my former employer, the Directorate of Operations of the CIA.

In a corner of the top-secret facility put into the basement of a building in Quantico, Virginia, I placed a single computer with access to the Internet. In that time, 1988, "the Internet" had not developed and was not as common as it became in the 1994–1996 timeframe, when individuals rather than organizations became the primary drivers of Internet connectivity. In that earlier context, the Internet was relevant to Marine Corps intelligence largely because of a single service with the marketing title of "The Source," and as a means of access to commercial services then in gestation for the larger public, such as LEXIS-NEXIS and a handful of online information sources and databases.

Imagine my surprise, having spent $20 million to give our analysts the best workstations possible, including complete access to all secrets costing the taxpayers billions, when I noticed the analysts standing in line for the one computer with Internet availability.

When I inquired, I learned that despite having complete access to all available secrets (which turned out to be extremely limited, neither "all" nor in many cases actually "secret"), the intelligence services did not process, scrutinize, or analyze vast troves of information that could be collected on Third World places of concern to the U.S. Marine Corps—places like Burundi, Haiti, and Somalia. In other words, the U.S. intelligence community was not about and not capable of doing decision-support to the

Marine Corps. This is when I realized that the entire secret intelligence community was a "paper tiger"[4] that existed to channel money from the taxpayer to favored corporations (the ones paying off members of Congress), without being held accountable for actually producing intelligence!

I was stunned. In an instant, my belief in the efficacy of gathering secret information evaporated. I realized that we—the actual workers of U.S. government—were looking through the wrong end of the telescope. We were investing vast amounts of effort and energy in stealing specific classified information from "denied areas" such as China and Russia, while ignoring the vast amount of available open-source information about everywhere else. In this context (the context of information and intelligence) "open source" means information that is ethically and legally available to the public in more than 183 languages—information that the U.S. intelligence operation, with its obsession on secrecy, ignores. This includes information available from commercial sources, educational databases, social networks, and journalists in various regions.

Put in the bluntest possible terms, what I discovered was that the U.S. secret intelligence community was collecting only information it considered secret, while ignoring the eighty to ninety percent of the information in the world, in all languages, that was not secret. I understand why they do this now: they are under the mistaken impression that they are about secrets rather than decision-support (intelligence); and they believe that their consumers, who have access to all open sources, are responsible for their own collection, processing, and analysis of open sources of information.

Others have realized this before me (for example, the Ellsberg to Kissinger quote in Chapter 1), but I am the one who took that realization the next step and began creating a viable alternative to the secret dysfunctional world that right now consumes a percentage of taxpayer funds vastly disproportional to its efficacy. In fact, if you focus on the CIA's drone program for killing people without due process, violating all manner of international conventions, you could reasonably say that secret intelligence and secret operations are actually our own worst enemy.

What the secret world does not realize is that the consumers of intelligence do not understand how to achieve intelligence, which is the *result* of applying a process that demands enormous professionalization and discipline if it is to be effective as decision-support: requirements definition, collection management, single-source discovery and validation, multi-source fusion, automated and human processing, automated and human analysis, and finally, visualization and presentation to a human "decider." At this point the craft of creating a single image that takes thirty seconds to appreciate can lead to the "decider" reading the rest of the page in three minutes and "getting it," i.e., being able to use the intelligence gathered to arrive at an answer, or to avoid costs and gain advantage toward specific objectives.

In that moment of my realization, the modern Open-Source Intelligence (OSINT) movement was born in the sense that I, a single individual then in public service, decided to make it my life's mission to take the craft of intelligence (decision-support) to the next level. It became my goal to teach governments how to leverage open sources of information, and to recognize that all the instruments of national power—every Cabinet Department, every agency—needs intelligence support, and they need intelligence support that is public in nature.

Weaknesses in the World of Secret Intelligence

Fast forward to 2008: General Tony Zinni, USMC (Retired), is on record as stating that when he was Commander-in-Chief of the U.S. Central Command, he received, "at best," four percent of the information he needed from secret sources and methods—four percent![5] This four percent costs the taxpayer today more than $80 billion dollars a year, spent mostly on corporate vapor-ware (vast programs going through the motions that fail to deliver ostensibly desired capabilities), a waste that is compounded by employees and computers going through the motions of collecting vast amounts of information that is never analyzed or studied. The National Security Agency, for example, processes less than five percent of what it collects, and for most matters, less than one percent.[6] No one is held accountable for the cost of the collected material that is never processed or analyzed.

From 1988 to 1992, still a civil servant, I spent four years trying to get the secret intelligence world to focus on open-source intelligence. At the time—and still today in 2012 as I finalize this book—the U.S. intelligence community classifies the results of its minimalist OSINT activities, claiming that the mere fact that the U.S. government is interested in X, Y, or Z makes it "secret." I spent those four years, part of my total twenty years in direct public service, trying to show how information-sharing and harmonization of policies, purchases, and day-to-day behavior—especially overseas—could be substantially improved by doing decision-support that was *not* secret, meaning OSINT, with the obvious benefit that it could be shared with the public, with foreign governments, non-governmental organizations, and all others.[7]

As the second-ranking civilian in Marine Corps Intelligence, I was a member of a number of national-level committees, including the Foreign Intelligence Requirements and Capabilities Plan committee, and I was able to propose a shifting of attention toward open sources of information and the Third World. I was, however, ignored. Even when the full weight of the U.S. Marine Corps was behind an initiative—for example, to redirect one third of the National Intelligence Topics to the Third World and "most likely" conflicts instead of "worst case" conflicts (then the Soviet Union, today China)—the national security complex refused to budge.

In 1992, frustrated by the unwillingness of the secret bureaucracy to shift even a modicum of resources away from the denied-area targets (places such as China, Iran, and Russia where the CIA has no capacity to operate with impunity as it does everywhere else) to what is called Global Coverage (the other ninety-nine percent—a notable analogy to the modern Occupy movement), I prevailed on my flag officer, the Director of Intelligence for the U.S. Marine Corps, to allow me to organize a conference on OSINT.

The CIA—home of the Foreign Broadcast Information Service and hence the only real OSINT unit in the secret world—was nominally responsible for OSINT as it relates to secret sources and methods. CIA operatives said they would attend only if the conference were held at the secret level and only U.S. citizens with security clearances were permitted to attend. Recognizing the idiocy of this position, I appealed through channels to Admiral Bill Studeman, USN, then Deputy Director of Central Intelligence, and at his direction the CIA attended the first truly open-to-all, multinational conference in the history of the secret world. I expected a hundred and fifty participants, but about six hundred and fifty showed up, with about seventy-five of those being contractors signing up at the door in a wild panic over possibly missing out on the next "big thing." Also attending were fifteen Swedes led by Dr. Stevan Dedijer, the founding father of what was then called Business Intelligence.[8]

It is important to observe that business, competitive and/or commercial intelligence operations are not the same thing as industrial espionage. The first three are defined by their practitioners as being totally focused on the use of open sources and ethical methods. Today the definitions have morphed, and business intelligence refers to comparisons of the results of data-mining to internal information; competitive intelligence refers mostly to studying one's competitors; and commercial intelligence is the new term that integrates "360-degree awareness" with a commitment to carefully study public needs, public environments, and all possible opportunities, not just threats.

The conference took place over three days in early December 1992. Alvin Toffler was sent a copy of the *Proceedings* by a participant who knew him, and this became the foundation for his chapter, "The Future of the Spy," in *War and Anti-War: Survival at the Dawn of the 21st Century.*[9]

More than forty countries participated. I believe the very high level of participation was due to our openness to all comers, and the diversity that responded to that wide-ranging invitation. By being open, we attracted a diversity of viewpoints that the CIA had never been able to muster because its obsession with secrecy channels its work into "bilateral" relationships and very narrow information-sharing exchanges. I now realize that one reason the CIA fails so consistently is that it never gets a grip on the whole picture. Because of the fragmentation of knowledge and its separation into particular domains that do not communicate with each other, the CIA is down in the weeds, uncovering little secrets that are out of context, without a larger sense of the coherent whole. The CIA is also terribly dependent on foreign liaison services (the secret intelligence elements of other governments) for most of what it claims to have acquired via clandestine methods. Due to a hyper-focus on disconnected information, no one in the secret world has a grip on global reality, let alone the capacity to access crucial information in the 183 languages we do not understand. Decades later, I would help pioneer Information Operations (IO), which is best understood as all information in all languages meeting the needs of all people. Here is an unattributed quote that puts the relationship among secret intelligence, open intelligence, and information operations in context:

> Secret intelligence is ten percent of all-source intelligence, and all-source intelligence is ten percent of Information Operations.[10]

Here I will just emphasize that it includes public intelligence in the public interest, with the goal of synthesizing a vast amount of information to provide a meta-perspective on world affairs as well as decision-support to every person on every issue of importance to them. IO is something we can all do for ourselves (e.g., crowd-sourcing of answers), though in the U.S. government it has been corrupted to mean secret intelligence and secret control of all communications, to include even spying on every citizen without regard to the rule of law.

To my surprise, after the success of the December 1992 conference, when I went to obtain permission for a follow-on conference as I had for the first event,[11] the Marine Corps lawyers refused to allow me to organize another conference, claiming that a "reasonable man" would think the conference was successful because I was a civil servant abusing my position to influence others to attend. I resigned from a very promising civil service tenured position to become a one-man small business educating mostly governments about the urgency of their getting a grip on OSINT. It took me twenty years to realize that I should have focused on teaching the public how to do public intelligence in the public interest, not on teaching brain-dead organizations how to capture and then make secret what the public and most of their clients (whose needs are not being met now) need to know.[12]

OSINT Rises to the Challenge

In 1995 I was invited to testify to the Aspin-Brown Commission (formally known as the Commission on the Roles and Capabilities of the U.S. Intelligence Community). This Commission was created as a gesture after then Secretary of Defense Dick Cheney and then Senator John Warner (R-VA) conspired to destroy the National Security Act of 1992 as developed by the Senate Select Committee on Intelligence and the House Permanent Select Committee on Intelligence. As Senator Warner blatantly made clear, he would not stand for "right-sizing" anything based in Virginia because right-sizing was code for down-sizing.

The Commission did well. Its report and recommendations were sound, but easy to ignore. A series of Directors of Central Intelligence, including George "Slam Dunk" Tenet, refused to implement any changes of substance.

With respect to their inquires into OSINT, they had

four witnesses. Tony Lake, then National Security Advisor, testified behind closed doors but is said to have admitted that he called his friends directly to obtain alternative viewpoints unburdened by secret sources and methods. A representative from the David Sarnoff Laboratory in Princeton testified (I do not make this stuff up) that he was not sure what OSINT was, but high-definition television would make it better. A representative of the RAND Corporation then testified to the effect (remember this was in 1995) that everything the U.S. government needed to know was on the Internet and they knew where to find it.

Then I testified, introducing the members of the Commission (among whom former Congressman Lee Hamilton and General Lou Allen, USAF [Retired] were the most attentive) to the debilitation inherent in a narrow focus of secret sources and methods, and the opportunity costs of ignoring all that could be done with open sources and methods. I drew on my second graduate thesis, written for the University of Oklahoma, regarding what was collected by three overseas embassies where I had worked, concluding that Washington was operating on two percent of the available relevant information (collecting twenty percent overseas, in the process spilling eighty percent of that in how it was or was not sent back). At the end of the day General Allen asked me if I was willing to do a benchmark exercise, one man and a telephone against the entire U.S. secret world including the CIA, NSA, NRO, and the Defense Intelligence Agency, as well as the many other secret elements in the military, law enforcement, and so on. I agreed. He turned to Britt Snider, the Staff Director for the Commission, and said something along the lines of "Today is Thursday. By ten o'clock on Monday I want everything the secret world has on Burundi. Mr. Steele, you have until ten o'clock on Monday to prove your point."

I was on my way to Las Vegas for a conference, so I called my assistant and had her fax five telephone numbers to my hotel, and I spent Friday on the telephone begging for free support from five major commercial enterprises; later we added a sixth. By ten AM on Monday, this is what was delivered to the Commission:

- From **LEXIS-NEXIS,** the names and contact information for the top international journalists reporting on Burundi and Rwanda, each available for direct interview to elicit the eighty percent that journalists do not publish but is often the most valuable information, centered on corruption.
- From the **Institute for Scientific Information** in Philadelphia, citation analysis[13] identifying the top hundred (most frequently cited) scholars on Burundi and Rwanda, each in contact with the unpublished field experts, all of them available for interviewing, with unique ground-truth perspectives unachievable through secret sources and methods.
- From **Oxford Analytica** in the United Kingdom, twenty two-page executive summaries previously written for the most senior levels of government and industry on

the implications of the genocide and surrounding instability in Burundi and Rwanda, locally and for the rest of humanity.

- From **Jane's Information Group,** which kindly called in an analyst for the weekend, a complete order of battle for the armed unconventional tribes including descriptions of their "technicals" (e.g., Toyota pick-up trucks with mounted machine guns). At this time the CIA was still focusing on uniformed forces associated with collapsing governments, and had no idea how to assess the non-governmental forces in conflict.
- From **East View Cartographic** in Minneapolis, a complete inventory of Russian military 1:50,000 combat charts (maps) with contour lines. The U.S. government never took the Third World seriously and still today does not have usable maps for ninety percent of the world.

A few weeks later I was able to add SPOT Image, a French satellite imagery company, to my list of contributors. They had all of Burundi in satellite imagery at the 1:10 meter level (sufficient for updating 1:50,000 combat charts), cloud-free, and in the archives (cheaper than fresh collection).

The U.S. government was able to produce only a flawed regional economic study and a small bland map of the region. I knew they would fail going into the exercise for the simple reason that the secret world is completely inattentive to the Third World and to issues not having to do with "super-threats" (real and contrived). These "super-threats" at the time included China, Iran, and Russia. Government agencies obsess on "secrets for the President" and on the handful of "denied area" countries that are considered to be a nuclear threat; their work is worthless when it comes to providing decision-support on everything else to everyone else. Since 2001 government intelligence has obsessed on terrorist groups and the "Global War on Terror," a war that I, as a former spy on terrorists, once described on Fox television as a fake war. I was not invited back.

Over the next seventeen years, as Chief Executive Officer for Open-Source Solutions Network, Inc. (until 2010), with one full-time employee (me), I served as the Johnny Appleseed for OSINT. In the 1990s I introduced twenty governments to the concept through invited seminars within the host country, and over that time I also directly trained 7,500 mid-career officers from across sixty-six countries, influencing many others through a free online website.[14] There were two partial success stories, but only partial. They were a 2000 appearance at a NATO gathering (sixty-six generals and colonels who did *not* get it, but the host did) and a 1997 audience with General Peter Schoomaker, then Commander in Chief of the U.S. Special Operations Command. He got my point in less than five minutes and ordered the creation of what has proven to be the only effective OSINT unit in the U.S. government to date, J-23. For many years this branch answered forty percent of all intelligence requirements from across the entire global special-operations world for under $10 million annually.[15] Of the other sixty percent, I estimate that the secret world answered one third, and the other two thirds went unsatisfied, in large part because the secret world is much less capable than people realize.

As a side note, OSINT does not make all spying and secrecy obsolete. What it does do is raise the standard for government intelligence while demanding *that we produce intelligence for everyone.*[16]

In 2000, the North Atlantic Treaty Organization (NATO) invited me to brief all the heads of military intelligence across all the NATO countries as well as the Partnership for Peace countries, the latter consisting of Eastern European countries no longer in the Soviet orbit.

OSINT handbooks were written, one for the Defense Intelligence Agency, another for NATO, a third for the Special Operations Forces (Civil Affairs). Budget allocations for OSINT grew over time, but to my great distress, the concept of OSINT was corrupted immediately. Instead of actually nurturing direct open access to external experts with real language and cultural qualifications, the government bureaucracies I was dealing with allocated hundreds of millions of dollars to what we call "butts in seats"—citizens with clearances who surf the Web.[17]

The Co-Evolution of OSINT

In 2002 I found Tom Atlee through his book, *The Tao of Democracy: Using Co-Intelligence to Create a World That Works for All,*[18] and he subsequently spoke in 2004 to the multinational open source conference that I had started in

1992. If the failure of the secret world as manifested in the Marine Corps Intelligence Center had opened my eyes, Tom's book and his general representation of the culture of *co-evolution* that Stewart Brand, Howard Rheingold, and others pioneered in earlier decades gave me the light on the path.[19]

Co-evolution is a concept that embraces millennia of natural development, where both animal and plant life change and grow through complex ecologies of interactive support—they evolve *together*, to the point that one cannot live in isolation from the other (or more than one other). The bottom line: "community" is not an elective, it is a requirement for the evolution and survival of humanity. We have been deconstructing community for centuries and separating from nature, only to recognize now that our salvation as a species lies in reconnecting with our natural roots.

Because of Tom Atlee I began to read much more broadly, and over the course of a decade or more I have embraced several distinct clusters of advanced thinking. They form the foundation—the human shoulders upon which I stand as I offer this *Open-Source Everything Manifesto* in service to humanity. Three of these schools of thought focus on humanity, and two focus on Earth as a whole. My point in mentioning them involves the importance of open-source everything in context—our humanity, our Earth.

It is these five communities that have inspired me toward my latest emphasis: holistic analytics and multinational information-sharing and sense-making.

I credit Buckminster Fuller and Russell Ackoff with my

realization that instead of focusing on reforming govern-ment and how government does intelligence, I needed to focus on re-empowering the public, routing around government, and using public intelligence to harmonize all interested groups irrespective of their "organizational" character. Later it was Tom Atlee who connected me to the modern pioneers of co-creation. It took me twenty years to "absorb" what they were saying, as I gradually realized that I was—as Russell Ackoff puts it—striving to do the wrong thing righter (improve government) instead of doing the right thing (help the public self-govern).[20]

World Brain Community and Consciousness Community

Two of the communities draw in part from the work of French mystic Pierre Teilhard de Chardin, and they came together in the first manifesto from Evolver Editions, *Manifesto for the Noosphere: The Next Stage in the Evolution of Human Consciousness,* by Mayan scholar and visionary José Argüelles.[21] This book can be construed as a modern reclaiming of the age-old wisdom that asserts the holis-tic nature of life, the deep integration of individual con-sciousness with a cosmic consciousness, and the richness of paranormal, quantum, and even intra-terrestrial intel-ligence. Everything is alive—everything is connected—everything has a spirit—we are One, but only when we rise to the challenge of *being* One.

I think of the first of these two groups—the one focused on the World Brain as an objective—as the "World

Brain Community," a more Western, analytic/justice, data-oriented community that seeks to connect all human minds to all information in all languages all the time. Meanwhile, "Consciousness Community," the term I use for the second group—which is focused on elevating human consciousness as an objective—for me represents a more Eastern, intuitive, and spiritual, process-oriented community that seeks to restore all elements of the human spirit, reestablishing the balance between the male *techne* and the female *psyche*,[22] while better integrating humanity into both the natural time-energy cosmology of the Earth and the infinite cosmology of All.

Within the Consciousness Community I confess there are so many I do not know, having come to this community only in the past decade, but I single out Herbert Marcuse,[23] whom I studied in depth in the 1970s, and much more recently Tom Atlee, Barbara Marx Hubbard (*Conscious Evolution*), Juanita Brown and David Isaacs (*World Café*), Harrison Owen (*Wave Rider*),[24] and in the practical application arena, Sandy Heierbacher, pioneering catalyst of the National Coalition for Dialog and Deliberation.[25]

Within the World Brain Community I hold in the highest regard H.G. Wells (*World Brain*), Buckminster Fuller (*Ideas and Integrities*), Medard Gabel (*Designing a World that Works for All*), Hans Swegen (*Global Mind*), Howard Bloom (*Global Brain*),[26] and the more recent pioneers of the collective wealth, Alvin Toffler (*Revolutionary Wealth*), Barry Carter (*Infinite Wealth*), Yochai Benkler (*Wealth of Networks*), and Thomas Stewart (*Wealth of Knowledge*).[27]

There are many others, such as Russell Ackoff (*Redesigning Society*), John Warfield (*A Unified Systems Engineering Concept*), and in this era Kent Myers (*Reflexive Practice*).[28] These books are but a small sample of the 1,700-plus non-fiction books I have reviewed at Amazon, reading in ninety-eight categories.[29]

Dignity and Diversity Community

There is a third human-centric community that I think of as the Dignity and Diversity Community. Others call this group the Bottom of the Pyramid or the Three Billion Poor. This community understands that the one unlimited resource we have is the human brain, and that absent a global program to embrace, educate, and elevate those at the bottom of the pyramid, no amount of "consciousness" and no amount of "analytics" is going to create a prosperous world at peace. Here I want to single out just three in this community: Robert Fuller, Dee Hock, and C.K. Prahalad.[30]

The easiest way to understand the importance of this community is to combine two quotes, the first from Shervin Pishevar, founder of OpenMesh Project, and the second from James Bamford, a scholar-journalist who for decades has exposed the National Security Agency using only legal, ethical sources of information to illustrate the fraud, waste, and abuse that the NSA actually is (spending as it does vast sums of the citizens' hard-earned money without actually contributing any intelligence of note to anyone including the President).

Humans are the routers.

Eventually NSA may secretly achieve the ultimate in quickness, compatibility, and efficiency—a computer with petaflop and higher speeds shrunk into a container about a liter in size, and powered by only about ten watts of power: the human brain.[31]

Bioneers Community and Ecological Economics Community

The next two communities among my valued resources are the Bioneers Community and the Ecological Economics Community. I know too few of the Bioneers but deeply admire all they have done, and particularly those who have pioneered Bio-Mimicry, defined as our acknowledgement of intra-terrestrial intelligence, including our understanding that the Earth and its natural systems have vastly more "sense" ingrained in their every atom than we have as a species. Bio-Mimicry is our path back to integral consciousness.

In the Ecological Economics Community I single out Herman Daly (*Ecological Economics*, *For the Common Good*), who developed valuation methods leading to "true cost" economics. Among many others who followed related but distinct paths are Paul Hawken (*Ecology of Commerce, Natural Capitalism*) and most recently Charles Eisenstein (*Sacred Economics*).[32]

The Role of Hackers

Let me explain the role that hackers, as well as the act and ethos of hacking, have played in radicalizing my vision and showing me the absolute need for an *Open-Source Everything Manifesto*.

By coincidence or divine circumstance, different groups converged on "open" in the 1980s and 1990s. Open software was the biggest of the movements, showing tangible value from its beginning. In my view, citing Richard Stallman as an example, open software can be considered a huge "hack." Stallman has been honored by Hackers on Planet Earth (HOPE) and is widely considered to be a hacker. In the specific case of HOPE, he is recognized for having broken the back of corporate ownership of the software commons, enabling billions of people to enjoy the capabilities of software—and to contribute their cognitive surplus toward improving that open-source software—so as to create a multi-billion-dollar industry that is open and very much in the public interest.[33]

A good "hack" is doing something better than it has ever been done before, with fewer resources. Hackers are like astronauts, pushing the edge of the envelope, going where others have not gone before, or have gone in a wasteful or unproductive manner. Good hackers are able to find flaws in commercial software based on their superior skills in relation to those who coded the software in the first place. Hacking is good. It keeps the cutting edge sharp. Anyone who does not understand that is part of the industrial-era baggage that is holding us back.[34]

Hackers see things that others do not. For this reason, they are not only very good at creating elegant, lean code, but they are equally adept at finding flaws in code, and particularly flaws that would allow an unauthorized person to take over or exploit the code without others knowing—generally with some financial loss incurred by the firm being violated.

As an intelligence professional formerly in the civil service of the U.S. government, I was among the early pioneers in seeing the severe dangers of proliferating buggy software. I was a member of the national Information Handling Committee, and I recall a major national security agency, very competent in the software arena, briefing us to the effect that in one year they found more than five hundred embedded Trojan Horses, viruses, and forms of malicious mischief in shrink-wrapped software and hardware arriving at their loading dock. In 1994 I wrote the original letter to Marty Harris, then in charge of the National Information Infrastructure, warning of the dangers and providing a $1 billion a year proposal[35] that drew on the deep knowledge of Jim Anderson at the National Security Agency, Winn Schwartau (author of *Terminal Compromise* and *Information Warfare: Chaos on the Electronic Superhighway*), and Bill Caelli, a professor based in Australia and along with Jim and Winn, one of the top people at the time in the emergent arena of computer security.

This matters because the U.S. government ignored us, just as the U.S. Congress ignored Winn when he testified in 1990–1991 on the coming tsunami of bad code and huge flaws in all systems. Had they listened, instead of spending $15 billion a year today for the Cyber-Command and a range of poorly conceptualized, poorly designed, and very badly implemented programs, we would today have an open-source cyber-solution in place, with all bugs being quickly eradicated through the application of the open-source everything philosophy.

It was Winn Schwartau who recommended me to HOPE. I was the very first speaker in 1994, and I've been invited back to speak at every conference since then (they are held every two years). In the same time frame, I was elected (it is an honorary society) to the Silicon Valley Hackers Conference started by Stewart Brand and have been part of that community ever since.

Hackers have the "right stuff." Hackers are about integrity combined with intelligence. Integrity in the hacker sense is concerned with transparency, truth, and trust, and with feedback loops that are complete, uncorrupted, and visible. Integrity involves seeing the whole, appreciating the whole, and respecting the nuances and complexities of the whole—in other words, *Integrity at Scale,* the title of a book by Steven Howard Johnson.[36] Just as we are now shifting from an Industrial Era sense of self as "ME the Consumer" toward a Cosmic Era sense of self as "WE the Community," so also do hackers change the "design culture" of a society. Occupy is a culture hack, not a political or economic movement.[37]

166

I am a patriot. I have always sought to serve my country, in theory a Republic. Learning that secrecy was evil rather than good was my first step. From there it was a steady march toward open-source everything. Now I see all the evil that secrecy enables in a corrupt Congress, a corrupt Executive, a corrupt economy, and a corrupt society. I see that the greatest service I or any other person can render to the Republic is to march firmly, non-violently, toward open-source everything. Winston Churchill had it right when he famously gave a university speech, striking the lectern three times with his walking stick, repeating each time with clarity and integrity: "Never Give Up."

BigBatUSA: We the People Reform Coalition

This is a model for what an honest, intelligent presidential candidate should offer. We should not be electing anyone who cannot produce a coalition cabinet and balanced budget in advance of election and via transparent means. We should be looking for a president who can eliminate the tax burden on all Americans, while also standing firmly for True Cost Economics. We should be looking for a president committed to zero inflation and full employment for all U.S. citizens. We should be looking for a president who upholds the Constitution and the sovereign will of the people over that of the bureaucracies and crime families.

http://bigbatusa.org

Phi Beta Iota the Public Intelligence Blog

This is the front end for 30 years of effort by more than 800 top experts on public intelligence, with links to the 30,000 pages at Open-Source Solutions Network, Inc. (www.oss.net) and the now quiescent Earth Intelligence Network (www.earth-intelligence.net).

www.phibetaiota.net

Free Online Guides to "Doing" Intelligence

    Articles & Chapters
    Briefings & Lectures
    Books
    Graphics
    Handbooks
    Historic Contributions
    Journal of Public Intelligence
    Letters of Note
    Reviews of Non-Fiction Books

Above are principal headings at *Phi Beta Iota*, which appear in the middle column on the website. The right-hand column has "Most Popular" across various categories. Everything you need to "do" public intelligence in the public interest is here.

My email is robert.david.steele.vivas@gmail.com. I live to see the day when we restore the Republic.

ENDNOTES

Foreword

1. Julian Assange is the editor-in-chief and founder of *WikiLeaks*, the website publication that leaked hundreds of thousands of documents from U.S. military communications, including Department of State communications.

2. WikiLeaks began releasing U.S. military documents in July 2010. It dumped the entire archive of diplomatic documents in September 2011. A recent story is "WikiLeaks scandal sparks U.S. intelligence reform," *Agence-France Presse,* 27 January 2012. I can assert that no such reform has actually occurred. It is not possible to reform how the U.S. "does" communications because their legacy systems ignored the work that I did within CIA in 1986–1988, and outside the CIA in 1990–1994. My 1994 letter to the head of the National Information Infrastructure can be viewed online at "1994 Sounding the Alarm," at www.phibetaiota.net/1994/08/1994-sounding-the-alarm-on-cyber-security/.

3. Linda J. Bilmer and Joseph E. Stiglitz, *The Three Trillion Dollar War: The True Cost of the Iraq Conflict* (New York: W.W. Norton & Company, 2008); "Afghan Civilians Killed in Offensive on Taliban," *ProgressNow Colorado,* 15 February 2010; and Rick Maze, "18 veterans commit suicide each day," *Army Times,* 22 April 2010.

Author's Preface

1. Norman Cousins, *The Pathology of Power* (New York: Norton, 1987).

2. Learn more at www.phibetaiota.net/m4is2/.

3. Alvin Toffler, *PowerShift: Knowledge, Wealth, and Violence at the Edge of the 21st Century* (New York: Bantam, 1991).

4. Integrity is about much more than personal honor. In a systems context, it is about truth and completeness. Lies are "friction" and lead to loss. Missing information is a form of friction and also leads to loss.

5. *Cf.* Pierre Levy, *Collective Intelligence: Mankind's Emerging World in Cyberspace* (New York: Basic Books, 1999); Mark Tovey (ed.), *Collective Intelligence: Creating a Prosperous World at Peace* (Oakton, VA: Earth Intelligence Network, 2008); Howard Rheingold, *Smart Mobs: the Next Social Revolution* (New York: Basic Books, 2003); James Surowiecki, *The Wisdom of the Crowds* (New York: Anchor, 2005); Glenn Reynolds, *An Army of Davids: How Markets and Technology Empower Ordinary People to Beat Big Media, Big Government, and Other Goliaths* (New York: Thomas Nelson, 2007); Clay Shirky, *Here Comes Everybody: The Power of Organizing Without Organizations* (New York: Penguin, 2009); and Charlene Li and Josh Bernoff, *Groundswell: Winning in a World Transformed by Social Technologies* (Cambridge, MA: Harvard Business Review Press, 2011).

6. Buckminster Fuller, *Synergetics: Explorations in the Geometry of Thinking* (New York: Macmillan Publishing Company, 1982).

7. Col John Boyd, USAF (Ret.), is the originator of this concept. It is at the heart of the Occupy movement's disdain for hierarchical organizations precisely because hierarchies are not able to Observe, Orient, Decide, and Act with near-real-time efficiency. They are cumbersome and corrupt. In contrast, civil society, when properly facilitated in the form of Citizen Wisdom Councils or deliberative dialog

networks, is astonishingly agile as well as reliable in draw-ing correct actionable conclusions that minimize loss of time and use of resources while achieving outcomes satis-factory to most: the very concept of democracy.

8. "U.S. intelligence budget tops $80 billion," UPI.com, 28 October 2010.

9. This quote came to me from a Colonel close to General Zinni, and was formally published in my article on "Open-Source Intelligence" in the six-volume set edited by Dr. Loch Johnson, *Strategic Intelligence* (Santa Barbara, CA: Praeger, 2006), Volume II, Chapter 6, pp. 95–122, quote on p. 98. The complete quote can be seen in a single "Graphic: Tony Zinni on 4% 'At Best,' at www.phibetaiota .net/2010/12/graphic-tony-zinni-on-4-at-best/. I subse-quently published an article on this theme, "Intelligence for the President—AND Everyone Else" (*Counterpunch*, Weekend Edition, Feb 29–Mar 02, 2009).

10. Among my various books, one in particular was written for the public, *THE NEW CRAFT OF INTELLIGENCE: Personal, Public & Political—Citizen's Action Handbook for Fighting Ter-rorism, Genocide, Disease, Toxic Bombs, and Corruption* (Oak-ton, VA: OSS International Press, 2002).

11. I first wrote about this concept in "Creating a Smart Nation: Strategy, Policy, Intelligence, and Information," *Government Information Quarterly*, Vol. 13, No. 2 (1996), pp. 159–174. Subsequently, with Congressman Rob Simmons (R-CT-02) writing the Foreword, I published *THE SMART NATION ACT: Public Intelligence in the Public Interest* (Oakton, VA: OSS International Press, 2006), as well as *INFORMATION OPERATIONS: All Information, All Languages, All the Time* (Oakton, VA: OSS International Press, 2006).

12. Two books contrast competing approaches, one tired, the other wired, to the general topic of open governance. The first, Daniel Lathrop and Laurel Ruma, *Open Government: Collaboration, Transparency, and Participation in Practice* (San Francisco: O'Reilly Media, 2010), is "tired." It takes government corruption in stride, ignores the two-party tyranny, and has no concept for strategic analytics. Its most revolutionary insight is that all government information should be open. The second, Paul Atkinson et al., *Open Design Now: Why Design Cannot Remain Exclusive* (Amsterdam, NL: BIS Publishers, 2011), is "wired." Reviewed by Michel Bauwens of the P2P Foundation, among others, this latter book illuminates the core attribute of the post-industrial era (or "Epoch B"): open-source everything.

13. If the secret world is the poster child for dysfunctional government, then Monsanto, along with Exxon, Wal-Mart, and Goldman Sachs, is the poster child for dysfunctional commerce. Water is the next frontier for predatory corporations. The time to put a stop to all of these crimes against humanity and nature is now.

14. Occupy is a global movement that is not affiliated with a specific political party and indeed rejects all corrupt forms of organization, among which the two dominant parties in the USA would certainly be counted. The Tea Party is unique to the USA and closely identified with the Republican Party.

15. The Republicans and Democrats have conspired with the blocking of ballot access, gerrymandering, electoral fraud, and campaign finance corruption, in order to exclude all six of the other accredited political parties: Constitution, Green, Libertarian, Natural Law, Reform, and Socialist.

174

The Natural Law and Socialist parties are not active at this time, but still accredited. The Libertarian Party claims it is the third-largest party in the U.S.; globally the Greens are the larger body. Many books have discussed the tyrannical nature of the two-party monopoly of power. Two of the better ones are Peter Petersen, *Running on Empty: How the Democratic and Republican Parties Are Bankrupting Our Future and What Americans Can Do About It* (New York: Picador, 2005), and Theresa Amato, *Grand Illusion: The Myth of Voter Choice in a Two-Party Tyranny* (New York: The New Press, 2009). See also Robert Steele, *ELECTION 2008: Lipstick on the Pig* (Oakton, VA: Earth Intelligence Network, 2008).

16. *Cf.* Charles C. Mann, *1491: New Revelations of the Americas Before Columbus* (New York: Vintage, 2006).

17. The original 60 slides, in color, for this book, can be viewed as a slide show at *Phi Beta Iota the Public Intelligence Blog*, www.phibetaiota.net/2011/10/2012-manifesto-for-truth-intelligence-with-integrity-in-the-public-interest-evolver-editions-july-2012/.

Chapter 1: Open Sesame

1. This is based on Purin Phanichphant, "Pyramid version of Open-Source Everything visualization," as posted by Michel Bauwens at the P2F Foundation website, 18 October 2009.

2. When Ron Paul appeared on video speaking the memorable words in Congress, "Lying is not patriotic," I was moved to connect the video and the nine questions he asked with nine answers I composed, and links to four books on the pathologies of secrecy, and two books on our missing democracy. Robert David Steele, "Empire of Lies and Secrecy," *Huffington Post*, 11 December 2011.

3. Devised by Lawrence Lessig, Creative Commons is a means of enabling complete open sharing while reserving some rights, for example, the right to financial profit. Their motto is "The Power of the OPEN." Learn more at http://creativecommons.org.

4. *Cf.* Karl Denninger, *LEVERAGE: How Cheap Money Will Destroy the World* (New York: Wiley, 2012).

5. *Cf.* Transition United States at http://transitionus.org, and Transition Network UK, at www.transitionnetwork.org.

6. I coined this term to describe what we need to develop rapidly as we see more signs of the U.S. government being part of a criminal corporate network intent on censoring and controlling the Internet, and inspired by what was done in Egypt to create work-arounds after the government sought to turn off the Internet. Working with Michel Bauwens, we created the Autonomous Internet Road Map, http://p2pfoundation.net/Autonomous_Internet_Road_Map.

7. EarthGame™ is a registered trademark of Medard Gabel, co-creator with Buckminster Fuller of the analog world game. His early work and the trademark fees were funded by Earth Intelligence Network, but he retains complete ownership of his intellectual property. Global Game is the generic term for the combination of the human network, the totality of the information in many languages and mediums, and all the functionalities.

8. There are too many great minds to list here. Instead I have created two lists of reviews, one of thinkers highlighting the negative aspects of what we do, the other highlighting the thinkers outlining the positive possibilities of what we might do. Both lists can be found at www.phibetaiota.net/reviews or search via their names—Worth a Look: Book

Review Lists (Negative); and Worth a Look: Book Review Lists (Positive).

9. This is included in Richard Stallman's Wikipedia biography, with documentation. See http://en.wikipedia.org/wiki /Richard_Stallman.

10. The single best illumination of this point is offered by James Bamford, *Body of Secrets: Anatomy of the Ultra-Secret National Security Agency* (New York, Anchor, 2002). The very last sentence in his book merits sharing here:

> Eventually NSA may secretly achieve the ultimate in quickness, compatibility, and efficiency—a computer with petaflog and higher speeds shrunk into a container about a liter in size, and powered by only about ten watts of power: the human brain.

11. C.K. Prahalad, *The Fortune at the Bottom of the Pyramid: Eradicating Poverty Through Profits* (Upper Saddle River, NJ: Pearson Prentice Hall, 2009), opened my eyes to the FACT that the five billion poor have an aggregate annual income of four trillion, FOUR TIMES the aggregate annual income of the one billion rich. If we can overcome the corruption of our governments, banks, and corporations, capitalism should enjoy an extraordinary renaissance, as Howard Bloom has forecast in *The Genius of the Beast: A Radical Re-Vision of Capitalism* (Amherst, NY: Prometheus Books, 2011). The idea that sheer human brain power—average human brain power—could create infinite wealth came to me from Barry Carter, *Infinite Wealth: A New World of Collaboration and Abundance in the Knowledge Era* (Burlington, MA: Butterworth-Heinemann, 1999). He was coincident with Alvin Toffler in *PowerShift: Knowledge, Wealth, and Violence at the Edge of the 21st Century* (New York: Bantam, 1991), and years ahead of the next big book along these lines,

Yochai Benkler, *The Wealth of Networks: How Social Production Transforms Markets and Freedom* (New Haven, CT: Yale University Press, 2007).

12. See note 3, above.

13. This is the conclusion of my briefing and then chapter in support of a Danish conference on counter-terrorism. Terrorism is a TACTIC and it is a symptom of deep social disease caused by an imbalance of power and wealth in any given society. Learn more at Robert David Steele, "The Ultimate Hack: Re-inventing Intelligence to Re-engineer Earth," in U. K. Wiil (ed.), *Counterterrorism and Open Source Intelligence* (Dusseldorf, Germany: Springer-Verlag, 2011).

14. Apart from many articles and chapters, the key books I have written, edited, or published include *ON INTELLIGENCE: Spies and Secrecy in an Open World* (Fairfax, VA: Armed Forces Communications and Electronics Association, 2000); *THE NEW CRAFT OF INTELLIGENCE: Personal, Public & Political* (Oakton, VA: OSS International Press, 2002); co-editor, *PEACEKEEPING INTELLIGENCE: Emerging Concepts for the Future* (Oakton, VA: OSS International Press, 2003); *INFORMATION OPERATIONS: All Information, All Languages, All the Time* (Oakton, VA: OSS International Press, 2006); *THE SMART NATON ACT: Public Intelligence in the Public Interest* (Oakton, VA: OSS International Press, 2006); Publisher: *COLLECTIVE INTELLIGENCE: Creating a Prosperous World at Peace* (Oakton, VA: Earth Intelligence Network, 2008); and *INTELLIGENCE for EARTH: Clarity, Diversity, Integrity & Sustainability* (Oakton, VA: Earth Intelligence Network, 2010).

15. I am a huge admirer of Barbara Marx Hubbard, and it was from her various books, DVDs, and website that I realized

that the Mayan long-count calendar set 22 December 2012 as an epochal shift. While many fear the worst, I believe we are being tested, and we have the capacity to surge our collective human intelligence and our collective human spirituality, and break free from the corrosive customs of the previous epoch. (The differences are illustrated in Figure 4.)

16. Tom Atlee, *The Tao of Democracy: Using Co-Intelligence to Create a World that Works for All* (Charleston, SC: BookSurge Publishing, 2002).

17. Tom Atlee, *Reflections on Evolutionary Activism: Essays, Poems and Prayers from an Emerging Field of Sacred Social Change* (Scotts Valley, CA: CreateSpace, 2009). See also his newer book (which makes a fine follow-up to *The Open-Source Everything Manifesto*), *Empowering Public Wisdom: A Practical Vision of Citizen-Led Politics* (Berkeley, CA: Evolver Editions, 2012).

18. Beginning with my own understanding of secrecy versus openness, I was inspired to create Figure 4 by Jonas Salk, *The Survival of the Wisest* (Harper & Row, 1973); Kirkpatrick Sale, *Human Scale* (New Catalyst Books, 2007); and E. F. Schumacher, *Small is Beautiful: Economics as if People Mattered* (Harper & Row, 1975).

19. Two recent books that document how Washington makes decisions directly contrary to available information are Joshua Rovner, *Fixing the Facts: National Security and the Politics of Intelligence* (Ithaca, NY: Cornell University Press, 2011), and Paul Pillar, *Intelligence and U.S. Foreign Policy: Iraq, 9/11, and Misguided Reform* (New York: Columbia University Press, 2011).

20. This is a reference to Max Weber, whose work is rooted in

German traditions and the study of sociology. He defined bureaucracy, capitalism, and religions in relation to hierarchies of command and control that included the hoarding of knowledge at each level and within each "silo." In today's environment, as David Weinberger explains so brilliantly in *Everything is Miscellaneous: The Power of the New Digital Disorder* (New York: Holt Paperbacks, 2008), information is no longer valuable when it is hoarded; it acquires its greatest value when it is shared many times over.

21. I do not address the literature on the abuse of secrecy as well as the natural but pathological competition among bureaucratic elements that hoard information for selfish ends rather than sharing information for the "good of the group." This manifesto focuses primarily on the conflict between a government prone to Epoch-A behavior and a public that deserves—and is capable of achieving—Epoch-B processes and outcomes.

22. Rather than list a few of the many books on these topics, let me point only to my two master lists of book reviews, at www.phibetaiota.net/reviews/.

23. Rather than list a variety of references, the reader can simple search for "corruption is endemic" and browse the 600,000 hits that result.

24. One of the most promising ideas within the Smart Nation Act is that of establishing an Office of Information-Sharing Treaties and Agreements within the Department of State.

25. Daniel Ellsberg, *SECRETS: A Memoir of Vietnam and the Pentagon Papers* (New York: Viking, 2002). This is his recollection of his words to Henry Kissinger, then National Security Advisor to President Richard Nixon. The three pages on the pathological effects of falling prey to the cult

of secrecy, on pages 237–239, should be forced rote memorization for all who receive security clearances.

26. Ben Gilad, *Business Blindspots: Replacing Your Company's Entrenched Assumptions and Outdated Myths, Beliefs, and Assumptions with the Realities of Today's Markets* (Chicago: Probus Professional Publications, 1993), p. 1.

27. Search for < Autonomous Internet Roadmap >.

28. I helped create the Autonomous Internet Roadmap at the P2P Foundation, http://p2pfoundation.net/Autonomous _Internet_Road_Map (accessed 15 February 2012).

29. Two useful books on this concept—but devoid of understanding of collective intelligence and advances being made in information-sharing and analysis technologies, are Wolfgang Reinicke and Michael Armacost, *Global Public Policy: Government Without Government* (Washington, DC: Brookings Institution Press, 1998), and Wolfgang Reinicke et al., *Critical Choices: The United Nations, Networks, and the Future of Global Governance* (Ottawa, ON: IDRC Books, 2000). I was unaware, until searching for the above two books, that there was an earlier book on this topic by James Rosenau and Ernst-Otto Czempiel, *Government without Government: Order and Change in World Politics* (Cambridge, UK: Cambridge University Press, 1992). At a practical level, the best book I have found to date on actually "doing" global governance "around" government is Ken Conca, *Governing Water: Contentious Transnational Politics and Global Institution Building* (Cambridge, MA: The MIT Press, 2005).

30. See note 20 above and note 49 for Weinberger references.

31. See note 5, Author's Preface.

32. Larry Beinhart, *Fog Facts: Searching for Truth in the Land of Spin* (New York: Nation Books, 2006). *See also* Roger

Shattuck, *Forbidden Knowledge: From Prometheus to Pornography* (New York, NY: Mariner Books, 1997).

33. Robert Parry, *Lost History: Contras, Cocaine, the Press and 'Project Truth'* (Chicago: Media Consortium, 1999).

34. Stephen R. Weissman, "Censoring American Diplomatic History," *American Historical Association*, September 2011.

35. See also Gary Webb, *Dark Alliance: The CIA, the Contras, and the Crack Cocaine Explosion* (New York: Seven Stories Press, 1999).

36. Edward S. Herman and Noam Chomsky, *Manufacturing Consent: The Political Economy of the Mass Media* (New York: Pantheon, 2002).

37. Sheldon Wolin, *Democracy Incorporated: Managed Democracy and the Specter of Inverted Totalitarianism* (Princeton, NJ: Princeton University Press, 2010).

38. Bill McKibben, *The Age of Missing Information* (New York: Random House, 2006).

39. Jacques Ellul, *Propaganda: The Formation of Men's Attitudes* (New York: Vintage, 1973).

40. Jim Marrs, *Rule by Secrecy: The Hidden History That Connects the Trilateral Commission, the Freemasons, and the Great Pyramids* (New York: William Morrow, 2001).

41. "The 935 Lies They Told Us About Iraq," *truthdig*, 23 January 2008. See also Sheldon Rampton and John Stauber, *Weapons of Mass Deception: The Uses of Propaganda in Bush's War on Iraq* (London, UK: Hodder, 2003).

42. *Cf.* Linda J. Bilmes and Joseph E. Stiglitz, *The Three Trillion Dollar War: The True Cost of the Iraq Conflict* (New York: W. W. Norton & Company, 2008).

43. Sheldon Rampton and John Stauber, *Weapons of Mass Deception: The Uses of Propaganda in Bush's War on Iraq* (New York: Tarcher, 2003).

44. During a London concert ten days before the 2003 invasion of Iraq, lead vocalist Maines said "We don't want this war, this violence, and we're ashamed that the President of the United States (George W. Bush) is from Texas." The statement offended many Americans, who thought it rude and unpatriotic, and the ensuing controversy cost the band half of their concert audience attendance in the United States. The incident negatively affected their career and led to accusations of the three women being "un-American," as well as hate mail, death threats, and the public destruction of their albums in protest. Source: Wikipedia/Dixie Chicks citing film "Shut Up and Sing," and "Dixie Chicks Shut Up and Sing in Toronto," MSNBC, seen 10 August 2006.

45. John Taylor Gatto, *Weapons of Mass Instruction: A Schoolteacher's Journey Through the Dark World of Compulsory Schooling* (Gabriola, BC: New Society Publishers, 2010).

46. *Cf.* Karen De Coster, "How the Public Schools Keep Your Child a Prisoner of the State," LouRockwell.com, 31 January 2012; and also "19 Crazy Things That School Children Are Being Arrested For In America," endoftheamerican-dream.com, undated.

47. *Ibid.*

48. Without getting too far afield, it is worth noting that there are more than 5,000 secessionist movements today, over 20 of them in the USA, among which Vermont's is the strongest. A great deal of today's unrest can be traced to the combination of imposed artificial political boundaries resulting from colonialism, and the degree to which capitalism has been predatory, creating a global class war in which our elites bribe their elites, and the elites screw their respective publics. I will cite only three books here; there

are many others. *Cf.* Phillip Allott, *The Health of Nations: Society and Law Beyond the State* (Cambridge, UK: Cambridge University Press, 2002); Jeff Faux, *The Global Class War: How America's Bipartisan Elite Lost Our Future—and What It Will Take to Win It Back* (Hoboken, NJ: Wiley, 2006); Eduardo Galeano, *Open Veins of Latin America: Five Centuries of the Pillage of a Continent* (New York: Monthly Review Press, 1997).

49. David Weinberger, *Too Big to Know: Rethinking Knowledge Now That the Facts Aren't the Facts, Experts Are Everywhere, and the Smartest Person in the Room Is the Room* (New York: Basic Books, 2012).

50. Without a strategic analytic model one cannot begin to measure and appreciate "cause and effect," nor can one harmonize multi-agency, multinational endeavors on a shared base of information and sense-making. To see the model created by the Earth Intelligence Network, search for < Reference Strategic Analytic Model for Creating a Prosperous World at Peace >.

51. The ten high-level threats were defined and prioritized by the High-Level Panel on Threats, Challenge, and Change and reported in their book study, also free online, *A More Secure World: Our Shared Responsibility* (New York: United Nations, 2004). The ten threats are, in this order, Poverty, Infectious Disease, Environmental Degradation, Inter-State Conflict, Civil War, Genocide, Other Atrocities, Proliferation, Terrorism, and Transnational Crime.

52. The twelve core policies were selected (by me) from looking at "Mandate for Change" books associated with the past four or five presidential transition teams; these are published by folks aspiring to be asked to join the Cabinet of the winning president. The twelve core policies, those most

consistently addressed but usually in isolation from one another, are Agriculture, Diplomacy, Economy, Education, Energy, Family, Health, Immigration, Justice, Security, Society, and Water. I include the concept of democracy and civil liberties in Society.

53. A page (at the top) is dedicated to M4IS2 at www.phibeta -iota.net.

54. This concept was developed by Alessandro Politi over dinner at the first international conference on "National Security and National Competitiveness: Open Source Solutions," in December 1992. He subsequently published "The Citizen as 'Intelligence Minuteman,'" *International Journal of Intelligence and Counterintelligence* (16/1, 2003).

55. Panarchy is the process, resilience is the outcome. *Cf.* Lance H. Gunderson and C. S. Holling (eds.), *Panarchy: Understanding Transformations in Human and Natural Systems* (Washington, DC: Island Press, 2001); and Brian Walker and David Salt, *Resilience Thinking: Sustaining Ecosystems and People in a Changing World* (Washington, DC: Island Press, 2006).

56. José Argüelles, *Manifesto for the Noosphere: The Next Stage in the Evolution of Human Consciousness* (Berkeley, CA: Evolver Editions, 2011).

57. *Cf.* Kevin Kelly, *Out of Control: The New Biology of Machines, Social Systems, and the Economic World* (New York: Basic Books, 1995).

58. Charles Hampden-Turner, *Radical Man: The Process of Psycho-Social Development* (New York: Anchor Books, 1971).

59. The health industry, which together with defense is consuming so much of the taxpayer dollar, was studied by PriceWaterhouseCoopers; their report *The Price of Excess*, documents that 50% of every health dollar is waste. I have

seen similar studies for agriculture/food, for defense, and for energy. More recently I discovered the work of Kevin Carson, "How Much of the Economy is Friction?," as published online by the P2P Foundation.

Chapter 2: Open-Source Everything

1. Charles Eisenstein's *Sacred Economics: Money, Gift, and Society in the Age of Transition* (Berkeley, CA: Evolver Editions, 2011).

2. As accessed on their website, www.opensource.org/, 27 January 2012.

3. As specified at www.opencontent.org.

4. The digital divide between the rich and the poor is a major continuing concern. Digitizing land records, for example, has led to the theft of land by companies and landlords skilled at exploiting the digital world, while placing the poor lacking such access at a major *new* disadvantage. An excellent discussion is provided by Scott Gilbertson, "Open Data's Access Problem, and How to Solve It," Webmonkey, 22 September 2010.

5. *Cf.* David Weinberger, "Why open spectrum matters: the end of the broadcast nation," in Mark Tovey (ed.), *COLLECTIVE INTELLIGENCE: Creating a Prosperous World at Peace* (Oakton, VA: Earth Intelligence Network, 2008). His book, *Everything is Miscellaneous: The Power of the New Digital Disorder* (Holt, 2008), expands on the theme.

6. http://opensourceecology.org.

7. http://vimeo.com/16106427.

8. OpenBTS is the open-source software/hardware combination that replicates cellular phone services using open spectrum, allowing the emergence of free and very low-

cost communications. Combined with mesh networks and other means of disconnecting from the government/tele-communications monopoly of the grid, OpenBTS is the foundation for "liberation technology" and is central to the release of humanity from the corrupt hierarchies and their "rule by secrecy" manipulations and predations.

9. Open-mesh networks extend the OpenBTS capability to provide servers and other capabilities while creating the ability for one local network to "hopscotch" through adjacent local networks to achieve a state, national, and global capability that is "off the grid" in relation to corporate, government, and proprietary or patent controls.

10. Seidman was speaking to the Open-Source Lunch Club on January 1, 1994. Her observations were subsequently reported in *OSS Notices* 94-001, dated February 21, 1994, and appeared in "Creating a Smart Nation: Strategy, Policy, Intelligence, and Information," *Government Information Quarterly,* Vol. 13, No. 2, p. 395.

11. The unclassified version of this report can be found by searching for < 1997 Sutton (U.S.) The Challenge of Global Coverage >.

12. To see the actual page, search for < Graphic: 9-11 Commission Open-Source Agency >.

13. In the first instance, Sean O'Keefe, then Deputy Director of OMB, agreed with the recommendation of Don Gessaman, then recently retired Associate Deputy Director for National Security, but left soon after to lead the National Space and Aeronautics Administration (NASA), and the initiative died. In the second instance, several senior civil servants at OMB briefed by Joe Markowitz and Robert Steele agreed that the initiative had merit and could be

funded, but required the support of a Cabinet Secretary or an agency head. They specifically agreed that the OSA should not be part of the U.S. secret intelligence world, but rather be open and ideally diplomatic as a general service.

14. Search for < 2004 Modern History of Public Intelligence and the Opposition >.

15. To see the exact wording of the email from Lawrence Lessig to Alec Ross, and all other related materials, visit < Open-Source Agency: Executive Access Point > at www.phibetaiota .net/2011/08/open-source-agency-executive-access-point/.

16. An excellent MindMap with links to more substance of most—not all—of the terms can be found online by searching for < Everything Open and Free MindMeister >.

17. *Cf.* Lawrence Lessig, "Open Code and Open Societies," keynote address to "Free Software—A Model for Society?" (Tutzing, Germany, 1 June 2000).

18. See Chapter 1, Note 29, for more on Open Governance.

19. This vital term is still evolving. One earlier definition from the past has focused on multiple competing and overlapping functional jurisdictions. For this manifesto, "panarchy" is defined as everyone has access to all relevant information and access to all relevant decision dialogs at all levels that they wish to be part of—democracy on steroids with global reach.

20. System of governance using consent-based decision-making among equivalent individuals.

21. A form of governance that recognizes that every individual is his or her own authority, and also a vital part of a larger composite organization. Authority is distributed, agile, and flexible.

22. World Wide Web Consortium (W3C).

23. DNA: Deoxyribonucleic acid containing genetic instruc-

tions used in the development and functioning of all known living organisms.

24. A useful six-page document is online, "Open Cloud Manifesto" (OpenCloudManifesto.org, Spring 2009).

25. Protestants who believe in the primacy of the Bible, complete separation of church and state.

26. Enlightened spiritual energy.

27. Originally a Hindu discipline training consciousness through exercise and position.

28. Michel Bauwens, *The Great Cosmic Mash-Up*, and also *The Next Buddha Will Be a Collective*. Both are quickly found with other useful summary material at the P2P Foundation website under Category: Spirituality.

Chapter 3: Manifesto

1. This term is explained with elegance by Robert Wright, *The Logic of Human Destiny* (New York: Vintage, 2001).

Chapter 4: Philosophical Concepts

1. Mr. Seelert was at the time Chairman of Saatchi and Saatchi Worldwide, based in New York City. This quotation was confirmed by a very attentive public relations element.

2. These two lines appeared also at the opening of this book. The first is an adaptation of the less applicable "given enough eyeballs, all bugs are shallow" from Eric Raymond. The philosophy is implemented in Eric Raymond's own mandate of "Release Early, Release Often," from his seminal 1997 essay *The Cathedral and the Bazaar.* The second quote is my own, a blend of John 8:32, "Ye shall know the truth and the truth shall set you free," and what I learned from Dr. Herman Daly, father of ecological economics, about "true cost" analytics.

3. Available at various online quotation sites, including Wiki-quote Lawrence of Arabia (film).

4. I must recognize Winston Maike (RIP), an extraordinary philosopher and researcher from Australia, who discovered the original motto, based on a mix of the U.S. Naval Academy motto and the CIA motto, and kindly corrected the Latin.

5. Will Durant, *Philosophy and the Social Problem* (Frisco, TX: Promethean Press, 2008, originally published in 1916).

6. Will and Ariel Durant, *The Story of Civilization* (New York: Mjf Books, 1993).

7. E.O. Wilson, *Consilience: The Unity of Knowledge* (New York: Vintage, 1999).

8. Several books are implied in this sentence. They include David Callahan, The *Cheating Culture: Why More Americans Are Doing Wrong to Get Ahead* (Mariner Books, 2004); Jim Marrs, *Rule by Secrecy: The Hidden History That Connects the Trilateral Commission, the Freemasons, and the Great Pyramids* (New York: Harper Paperbacks, 2001); and Matt Taibbi, *GRIFTOPIA: Bubble Machines, Vampire Squids, and the Long Con That is Breaking America* (Spiegel & Grau, 2010).

9. *Cf.* Steve McIntosh, *Integral Consciousness and the Future of Evolution* (Paragon House, 2007); and Tom Atlee, *Reflections in Evolutionary Activism: Essays, poems and prayers from an emerging field of sacred social change* (Scotts Valley, CA: CreateSpace, 2009).

10. Letter to W.T. Barry (1822-08-04).

11. Durant, *Philosophy and the Social Problem* (see note 5).

12. An entire section of this book on "The Great Conversation" was deleted in the editorial process, but here are four quotes that I consider essential to the concept of open-source everything, a concept I would implement by inte-

grating education, intelligence, and research at all levels from local to global.

First, the threat:

The death of democracy is not likely to be an assassination from ambush; it will be a slow extinction from apathy, indifference, and undernourishment.

Now the process:

A republic is a common education life in process. So Montesquieu said that as the principle of an aristocracy was honor, and the principle of a tyranny was fear, the principle of a democracy was education.

Then the objective:

[T]he essential ingredients of strength are trained intelligence, love of country, the understanding of its ideals, and such devotion to those ideals that they become a part of the thought and life of every citizen.

And finally, the grave concern:

We believe that the reduction of the citizen to an object of propaganda, private and public, is one of the greatest dangers to democracy.

From Robert Hutchins, *The Great Conversation: The Substance of a Liberal Education* (Great Books of the Western World, Volume 1, Encyclopedia Britannica, 1952). Quotes are from pages 80 (death of democracy), 64 (a republic is), 61 (strength of democracy), and xiii (we believe).

13. James Bamford, *Body of Secrets: Anatomy of the Ultra-Secret National Security Agency* (New York: Anchor, 2002).

14. C.K. Prahalad, *The Fortune at the Bottom of the Pyramid: Eradicating Poverty Through Profits* (Upper Saddle River, NJ: Pearson Prentice Hall, 2009).

15. *Cf.* Clay Shirky, *Cognitive Surplus: Creativity and Generosity in a Connected Age* (New York: Penguin Press, 2010).

16. *Cf.* Gregory Unruh, "Transparency: The Internet's Killer CSR App," *Huffington Post,* December 3, 2010 (www .huffingtonpost.com/gregory-unruh/transparency-the -internet_b_791796.html), and its follow-on commentary, "Reference: Transparency Killer App Plus 'Open-Source Everything' RECAP," at *Phi Beta Iota the Public Intelligence Blog* (www.phibetaiota.net/2010/12/reference-transparency -killer-app/).

17. Sherman Kent, *Strategic Intelligence for American World Policy* (Princeton, NJ: Princeton University Press, 1953).

18. www.phibetaiota.net/1992/07/2447/.

19. "Robert Steele, "Creating a Smart Nation: Strategy, Policy, Intelligence, and Information," *Government Information Quarterly* 13/2 1995 (www.phibetaiota.net/1995/07/1995 -giq-132-creating-a-smart-nation-strategy-policy-intelligence -and-information/); the World Brain as conceptualized by H. G. Wells in a book by that name has been a recurring theme in a number of books across the past fifty years. Earth Intelligence Network and its 24 co-founders are the first to actually create an implementable plan for achieving this objective.

20. Harrison Owen, *Wave Rider: Leadership for High Performance in a Self-Organizing World* (San Francisco: Berrett-Koehler Publishers, 2008).

21. Matt Taibbi, "How I Stopped Worrying and Learned to Love the OWS Protests," *Rolling Stone* (10 November 2011).

Chapter 5: Integrity, Lies, and Panarchy

1. This became clear to me after reading Buckminster Fuller's

Ideas and Integrities: A Spontaneous Autobiographical Disclosure (New York: The Macmillan Company, 1969).

2. The meeting in question was a discussion hosted by the Brookings Institute in Washington, DC, 27 September 2011, to hear MajGen Robert Scales, USA (Ret.), discuss shortfalls in small-unit warfare capabilities. His most memorable observation was that 4% of the force (the infantry) takes 80% of the casualties, yet we spend less than 1% of the total Pentagon budget on their equipment and capabilities needs. He calls this, rather memorably, a "cosmic incongruity." My detailed notes on the meeting (including a link to my Reflections on Integrity) are at *Phi Beta Iota the Public Intelligence Blog*, www.phibetaiota.net/2011/12/robert -steele-on-the-record-4-of-the-force-takes-80-of-the-casualties -receives-1-of-the-pentagon-budget/).

3. Dr. Russell Ackoff is one of a handful of pioneers of reflexive thinking. Among his works are the seminal manifesto, "Transforming the Systems Movement," 26 May 2004, and his book with Sheldon Rovin, *Redesigning Society* (Stanford, CA: Stanford Business Books, 2003). Three quotes and links to both the above works are at *Phi Beta Iota the Public Intelligence Blog;* search for < Reference: Russell Ackoff on Doing Right Things Righter >.

4. Free online, find both the chapters individually and the book as a whole at *Phi Beta Iota the Public Intelligence Blog,* search for < 2008 ELECTION 2008: Lipstick on the Pig >.

5. Cunningham, one of a handful of Navy aces in the Viet-Nam war, with five confirmed kills, ended up as a Congressman whose downfall was described by the *Washington Post* as "the most brazen bribery conspiracy in modern congressional history." That is not actually the case—Cunningham

was just stupider than most. With a tiny handful of exceptions, every Senator and every Representative charges the going rate—5% for delivering an earmarked program. Learn more about Cunningham at http://en.wikipedia.org /wiki/Duke_Cunningham. The 5% number comes from a personal disclosure to the author by a senior Senate staffer responsible for budget matters related to national security.

6. The story was widely reported. Here is one example, "Federal Government Claims Right to Lie for National Security," *mrshambles.com*, 29 October 2011, accessed 27 January 2012 (http://mrshambles.com/2011/04/29/federal-gov -ernment-claims-right-to-lie-for-national-security/).

7. See note 2 above.

8. This is precisely what Secretary of Defense Leon Panetta did in January 2012, cutting the Army and Marine Corps by over 30,000 positions that in relative terms cost a tiny fraction of 1%, while protecting hundreds of billions of dollars in waste on corporate vapor-ware and systems that are both ineffective and unaffordable, such as the F-35. *Cf.* Chuck Spinney, "F-35: Out of Altitude, Airspeed, and Ideas—But Never Money," *TIME,* 30 January 2012.

9. *Cf.* Gregory Unruh, "Transparency: The Internet's Killer CSR App," *Huffington Post,* 3 December 2010, and its follow-on commentary, "Reference: Transparency Killer App Plus 'Open-Source Everything' RECAP," at *Phi Beta Iota the Public Intelligence Blog.*

10. Fyodor Dostoevsky, *The Brothers Karamazov* (Salt Lake City: Project Gutenberg, 2009).

11. Ron Paul, "Lying is Not Patriotic," YouTube (5:23), as recorded on the floor of the House of Representatives, 9 December 2011. Summarized at *Phi Beta Iota the Public*

Intelligence Blog, under heading "Reference: Lying Is Not Patriotic—Ron Paul."

12. *Cf.* Susanna Hoffman and Anthony Oliver-Smith, *Catastrophe & Culture: The Anthropology of Disaster* (Santa Fe, NM: School for Advanced Research Press, 2002).

13. Robert Wright, *Nonzero: The Logic of Human Destiny* (New York: Vintage, 2001) provides an extraordinary discussion of civilization and culture at their best, rejecting zero-sum outcomes, and creating infinite wealth. Tom Atlee introduced me to this book.

14. Jock Gill: "Thirteen Big Lies—Needed Counter-Narrative," *Phi Beta Iota the Public Intelligence Blog*, 31 May 2011.

15. Jonas Salk is generally credited with first making the distinction between Epoch A ("top down") and Epoch B ("bottom-up") forms of leadership. See "Graphic: Epoch B Swarm Leadership," *Phi Beta Iota the Public Intelligence Blog*, 16 August 2010.

16. David Callahan, *The Cheating Culture: Why More Americans Are Doing Wrong to Get Ahead* (Mariner Books, 2004).

17. *Cf.* James McEnteer, *Shooting the Truth: The Rise of American Political Documentaries* (Santa Barbara, CA: Praeger, 2005), and at a global level, John J. Mearsheimer, *Why Leaders Lie: The Truth About Lying in International Politics* (Oxford, UK: Oxford University Press, 2011).

18. Learn more at http://contactcon.com/.

19. http://emergentbydesign.com/.

20. Stephen Few, the author of this slide, can be found at his blog, PerceptualEdge.com, where he publishes Visual Business Intelligence.

21. I have written a full-length monograph on this topic, *Human Intelligence: All Humans, All Minds, All the Time* (Carlisle, PA:

Strategic Studies Institute, 2010), free online at (www.strategicstudiesinstitute.army.mil/pubs/display.cfm?pubID=991).

Chapter 6: Whole-Systems Thinking

1. See, for example, David Korten, *The Great Turning: From Empire to Earth Communing* (Jersey City, NJ: Kumarian Press, 2006); and Jeremy Rifkin, *The Empathetic Civilization: The Race to Global Consciousness in a World of Crisis* (New York: Tarcher, 2009); and all the works of scholar and activist Joanna Macy.

2. *Cf.* Barbara Marx Hubbard, *Conscious Evolution: Awakening Our Social Potential* (Novato, CA: New World Library, 1998), and Tom Atlee, *Reflections on Evolutionary Activism: Essays, poems and prayers from an emerging field of sacred social change* (Scotts Valley, CA: CreateSpace, 2009).

3. See other notes: Chapter 5, note 3; and the Epilogue, notes 20 and 28.

4. This is a reference to the work of Charles C. Mann, *1491: New Revelations of the Americas Before Columbus* (New York: Vintage, 2006).

5. Thomas Homer-Dixon, *The Ingenuity Gap: Facing the Economic, Environmental, and Other Challenges of an Increasingly Complex and Unpredictable Future* (New York: Vintage, 2002).

6. Charles Perrow, *Normal Accidents: Living with High-Risk Technologies* (Princeton, NJ: Princeton University Press, 1999).

7. *Cf.* Charles Perrow, *The Next Catastrophe: Reducing Our Vulnerabilities to Natural, Industrial, and Terrorist Disasters* (Princeton, NJ: Princeton University Press, 2011).

8. J. F. Richard, *HIGH NOON: 20 Global Problems, 20 Years to Solve Them* (New York: Basic Books, 2003).

   Group One: Sharing Our Planet: Global Warming, Biodiversity & Ecosystem Losses, Fisheries Depletion, Deforestation, Water Deficits, Maritime Safety & Pollution

Group Two: Sharing Our Humanity: Poverty, Peacekeeping & Conflict Prevention, Terrorism, Education for All, Infectious Diseases, Digital Divide, Natural Disaster Prevention & Mitigation

Group Three: Sharing Our Rule Book: Reinventing Taxation, Biotechnology Rules, Global Financial Architecture, Illegal Drugs, Trade-Investment-Competition Rules, Intellectual Property Rights & E-Commerce Rules, International Labor & Migration Rules

9. High-Level Panel on Threats, Challenges, & Change, *A More Secure World: Our Shared Responsibility* (United Nations, 2004). The threats, in priority order, are: Poverty, Infectious Disease, Environmental Degradation, Inter-State Conflict, Civil War, Genocide, Other Atrocities, Proliferation, Terrorism, Transnational Crime.

10. Tom Wessells, *The Myth of Progress: Toward a Sustainable Future* (Vermont: 2006).

11. Joseph Tainter, *The Collapse of Complex Societies* (Cambridge, UK: Cambridge University Press, 1990).

12. David Keys, *Catastrophe: An Investigation into the Origins of Modern Civilization* (New York: Ballantine Books, 2000).

13. Ted Steinberg, *Acts of God: The Unnatural History of Natural Disaster in America* (Oxford, UK: Oxford University Press, 2006).

14. Stewart Brand, *Clock of the Long Now: Time and Responsibility—The Ideas Behind the World's Slowest Computer* (New York: Basic Books, 2000).

15. The exact language, from the Constitution of the Iroquois Nations, includes the following sentence: "Look and listen

for the welfare of the whole people and have always in view not only the present but also the coming generations, even those whose faces are yet beneath the surface of the ground—the unborn of the future Nation." (Wikipedia, Seven generation sustainability, accessed 2 June 2011.)

16. Will and Ariel Durant, *The Lessons of History* (New York: Simon & Schuster, 2010).

17. Four books along these lines are Antoon De Baets, *Censorship of Historical Thought: A World Guide, 1945–2000* (New York: Greenwood, 2001); Robert Perry, *Lost History: Contras, Cocaine, the Press & 'Project Truth'* (Media Consortium, 1999); Larry Beinhart, *Fog Facts: Searching for Truth in the Land of Spin* (Nation Books, 2006); and Bill McKibben, *The Age of Missing Information* (New York: Random House, 2006).

18. Carol Gilligan, Janie War, Jill McLean, and Betty Bardige (eds.), *Mapping the Moral Domain: A Contribution of Women's Thinking to Psychological Theory and Education* (Cambridge, MA: Harvard University Press, 1990).

19. John Lewis Gaddis, *The Landscape of History: How Historians Map the Past* (Oxford, UK: Oxford University Press, 2004).

20. I credit this recollected thought to Howard Zinn, among whose works I especially appreciate *A Power Governments Cannot Suppress* (San Francisco: City Lights Publishers, 2006). I have not read but include here both the citation and a note about the book because it is so pertinent to the role of open-source everything and the 99%: *A People's History of the United States: 1492 to Present* (New York: Harper Perennial Modern Classics, 2005). This from *Publisher's Weekly* at Amazon: "According to this classic of revisionist American history, narratives of national unity and progress are a smoke screen disguising the ceaseless conflict between

elites and the masses whom they oppress and exploit. Historian Zinn sides with the latter group in chronicling Indians' struggle against Europeans, blacks' struggle against racism, women's struggle against patriarchy, and workers' struggle against capitalists. First published in 1980, the volume sums up decades of post-war scholarship into a definitive statement of leftist, multicultural, anti-imperialist historiography. . . . Zinn's work is a vital corrective to triumphalist accounts, but his uncompromising radicalism shades, at times, into cynicism. Zinn views the Bill of Rights, universal suffrage, affirmative action and collective bargaining not as fundamental (albeit imperfect) extensions of freedom, but as tactical concessions by monied elites to defuse and contain more revolutionary impulses; voting, in fact, is but the most insidious of the 'controls'."

21. Among the books that have most influenced my thinking in this arena, one stands out: E.O. Wilson, *Consilience: The Unity of Knowledge* (New York: Vintage, 1999).

22. Adapted from a figure in Steve Arnold, "Search panacea or ploy: Can collective intelligence improve findability?," in Mark Tovey (ed.), *COLLECTIVE INTELLIGENCE: Creating a Prosperous World at Peace* (Oakton, VA: Earth Intelligence Network, 2008). The Google portion has been added and is based on published knowledge about programmable search engines.

23. There are competing views on this point. The reference I draw on is Jack M. Hollander, *The Real Environmental Crisis: Why Poverty, Not Affluence, Is the Environment's Number One Enemy* (Berkeley: University of California Press, 2004). At the same time, corporations externalize over a third of their profits to the public. Here is just one reference on

this aspect, Juliette Jowitt, "World's top firms cause $2.2tn of environmental damage, report estimates," *The Guardian*, 18 February 2010.

24. In the intelligence world, domains are what the academics call "disciplines," and disciplines refer to collection sources and methods. Hence the primary disciplines in intelligence are Human, Imagery, and Signals, with Measurements & Signatures being a more esoteric discipline, and Open Source being both a discipline in its own right and a supporting discipline to all other disciplines. In this book domains are the academic specializations.

25. Colleen Scheck, "A Matrix of Science and Religion," *Being Blog*, undated.

26. Unsigned, "The Unification of Religion, Science, and Philosophy," *LAWWAI.com*, undated.

27. This graphic comes from Tim Kastelle, "Five Forms of Filtering," *Innovation Leadership Network*, with the diagram attributed to Harold Iarche. http://timkastelle.org/blog/2010/04/five-forms-of-filtering.

Chapter 7: Public Intelligence and the Citizen

1. Alessandro Politi coined this term over dinner at the first international conference on "National Security and National Competiveness: Open-Source Solutions," 6–8 December 1992, McLean, VA. He finally put his complete thoughts on this topic in writing, in "The Citizen as Intelligence Minuteman," *International Journal of Intelligence and Counterintelligence* 16/1 (Spring 2003). The full text can be viewed at www.phibetaiota.net/2003/03/2003-ijic-161-the-citizen-as-intelligence-minuteman/.

2. Among many books I would single out Malcolm Gladwell,

The Tipping Point: How Little Things Can Make a Big Difference (New York: Back Bay Books, 2002); Ori Brafman and Rod Beckstrom, *The Starfish and the Spider: The Unstoppable Power of Leaderless Organizations* (New York: Portfolio Trade, 2008); and Clayton Christensen and Michael Raynor, *The Innovator's Dilemma: Creating and Sustaining Successful Growth* (Cambridge, MA: Harvard Business School Press, 2003). I would temper these with such books as Stewart Brand's *Clock of the Long Now: Time and Responsibility—The Ideas Behind the World's Slowest Computer* (New York: Basic Books, 2000), and Rupert Sheldrake's *The Presence of the Past: Morphic Resonance and the Habits of Nature* (South Paris, ME: Park Street Press, 1995).

3. Three books stand out here, Howard Zinn, *A Power Governments Cannot Suppress* (San Francisco: City Lights, 2006); Vaclav Havel, *Power of the Powerless: Citizens Against the State in Central-Eastern Europe* (Armonk, NY: ME Sharpe Inc., 1985), and Jonathan Schell, *Unconquerable World: Power, Nonviolence, and the Will of the People* (New York: Holt, Henry & Co., 2003).

4. Alvin Toffler, *PowerShift: Knowledge, Wealth, and Violence at the Edge of the 21st Century* (New York: Bantam, 1991).

5. Pierre Teilhard de Chardin, *The Phenomenon of Man* (New York: Harper Perennial, 1976), and José Argüelles, *Manifesto for the Noosphere: The Next Stage in the Evolution of Human Consciousness* (Berkeley, CA: Evolver Editions, 2011).

6. I have reviewed most of the non-fiction books on Iraq. Those that are not blatant propaganda written by neo-conservatives generally agree that we went to war on the basis of 935 now-documented lies, most of which were refutable at the time, but the corporate media was bought

and paid for and actually refused (personal experience) fully-funded information advertisements against the war. One example of these books is James Bamford, *A Pretext for War: 9/11, Iraq, and the Abuse of America's Intelligence Agencies* (New York: Anchor Books, 2005). The lack of integrity at the highest levels (George "Slam Dunk" Tenet) repressed the integrity at lower levels. (Charlie Allen, the clandestine service, the analytic service—in this one instance they were uniformly correct and uniformly ignored. To understand how easily that is done, read Paul Pillar, *Intelligence and U.S. Foreign Policy: Iraq, 9/11, and Misguided Reform* [New York: Columbia University Press, 2011].)

7. It took J. Z. Liszkiewicz, Executive Director of the Earth Intelligence Network, almost one year to properly research the true cost of a cotton T-shirt. This included telephone calls all over the world. Learn more at http://true-cost .re-configure.org/true_cost_shirt.htm.

8. *Cf.* Herman Daly and Joshua Farley, *Ecological Economics: Principles and Applications* (Washington, DC: Island Press, 2003); Herman Daly and Kenneth Townsend (eds.), *Valuing the Earth: Economics, Ecology, Ethics* (Cambridge, MA: MIT Press, 1993); and Herman Daly and John Cobb, Jr., *For the Common Good: Redirecting the Economy toward Community, the Environment, and a Sustainable Future* (Boston: Beacon Press, 1994).

9. Robert David Steele, *The New Craft of Intelligence: Personal, Public & Political—Citizen's Action Handbook for Fighting Terrorism, Genocide, Disease, Toxic Bombs & Corruption* (Oakton, VA: OSS International Press, 2002).

10. Working with Congressman Rob Simmons (R-CT-02), a retired Army Colonel who single-handedly got both the Senate and the House of Representatives to understand the

importance of this endeavor, we drafted legislation called the Smart Nation Act. He was defeated for re-election and the opportunity was lost. *Cf.* Robert David Steele and Rob Simmons (Foreword), *The Smart Nation Act: Public Intelligence in the Public Interest* (Oakton, VA: OSS International Press, 2006).

11. (PriceWaterhouseCoopers, 2008), www.pwc.com/U.S./en /healthcare/publications/the-price-of-excess.jhtml.

12. Dr. Patrick Soon Shiong is a visionary with an estimated net worth of seven billion dollars; he has the means to build such a grid. In a demonstration of the open web, Gordon Cook (for 20 years proprietor of the COOK Report on Internet Protocol) did his own study of the Doctor's plans, which can be found at www.cookreport.com/patrick.pdf. In Gordon's opinion the Doctor would succeed if he openly explained what he is doing in detail and invited like-minded informed citizens to assist him. In addition to Gordon's report, learn more at http://duckduckgo.com /?q=Dr+Patrick+Soon+Shiong.

13. *Cf.* Robert D. Morris, *The Blue Death: The Intriguing Past and Present Danger of the Water You Drink* (New York: Harper, 2008); Robyn O'Brian, *The Unhealthy Truth: One Mother's Shocking Investigation into the Dangers of America's Food Supply—and What Every Family Can Do to Protect Itself* (Three Rivers Press, 2010); Ruth Winter, *A Consumer's Dictionary of Household, Yard, and Office Chemicals: Complete Information about Harmful and Desirable Chemicals Found in Everyday Household Products, Yard Poisons, and Office Polluters* (ASAJ Press, 2007); and Joseph Thorton, *Pandora's Poison: Chlorine, Health, and a New Environmental Strategy* (Cambridge, MA: MIT Press, 2001).

14. "Memoranda: Policy-Budget Outreach Tool," 17 December 2003, online at www.phibetaiota.net/2003/12/mem -oranda-policy-budget-outreach-tool/.

15. "Designing a Dashboard for 'Spaceship Earth'," *Haverford News*, 27 July 2009, at www.haverford.edu/news/stories /29321/51. Some illustrations of what such a dashboard might look like are online at http://earthdash.org/. See also www.earthshipdashboard.com.

16. *Cf.* Robert Horn, *Mapping Hypertext* (Arlington, VA: The Lexington Institute, 1989). This and related references inspired by Horn are online at www.phibetaiota .net/1989/08/reference-mapping-hypertext-1989/. See also Peter Morville, *Ambient Findability: What We Find Changes Who We Become* (Sebastopol, CA: O'Reilly Media, 2005).

17. These are discussed in detail in a chapter by the same name within Robert David Steele, *ELECTION 2008: Lipstick on the Pig* (Oakton, VA: Earth Intelligence Network, 2008). All chapters free online at www.phibetaiota.net/2008/07 /election-2008-lipstick-on-the-pig/.

18. The longer memorandum, "Citizen in Search of Integrity," is online at www.phibetaiota.net/2011/10/robert-steele-citizen -in-search-of-integrity-full-text-online-for-google-translate/.

19. Barry Carter, *Infinite Wealth: A New World of Collaboration and Abundance* (Burlington, MA: Butterworth-Heinemann, 1999).

20. My most recent book, *INTELLIGENCE for EARTH: Clarity, Diversity, Integrity, and Sustainability* (Oakton, VA: Earth Intelligence Network, 2010), is the "handbook" for creating the World Brain and Global Game. Shorter one-page, two-page, and longer briefings pertinent to this endeavor can be found at *Phi Beta Iota the Public Intelligence Blog* (www .phibetaiota.net),

21. This is a reference to Chris Hedges, *Empire of Illusion: The End of Literacy and the Triumph of Spectacle* (New York: Nation Books, 2010).

22. I learned this term from Karl Denninger, *LEVERAGE: How Cheap Money Will Destroy the World* (New York: Wiley, 2012).

23. "Jeff Bezos on the next web innovation," TED, filmed February 2003, posted April 2007, online at www.ted.com/talks /jeff_bezos_on_the_next_web_innovation.html. This is not the place to expand on intra-terrestrial intelligence, but I certainly encourage the reader to search for < intra-terres -trial intelligence >.

Epilogue: My Conversion Experience

1. I have written, edited, and published many articles, chapters, and books on this specific topic. The best way to access all that I and many others have created, free, is by using *Phi Beta Iota the Public Intelligence Blog,* which is also home to the very informal *Journal of Public Intelligence,* at www.phibetaiota.net.

2. At the time a colonel reporting to a brigadier general and a special assistant, Mr. John Guenther was the individual who put me forward for consideration. In the early 1990s the Director of Intelligence became a brigadier general position, reporting to a Major General responsible for Command, Control, Communications, Computing, and Intelligence (C4I). The following sentence, written by me for use by the Commandant to explain why the Marine Corps alone among the services integrated communications and intelligence, represents my frustration with the kum-ba-ya crowd that is all communications and no intelligence: "Communications without intelligence is noise;

intelligence without communications is irrelevant." Absent a unifying public intelligence network, all the advocacy groups will remain "noise."

3. Two deeply impressive books to read together are those by Ambassador Mark Palmer, *Breaking the Real Axis of Evil: How to Oust the World's Last Dictators by 2025* (Lanham, MD: Rowman & Littlefield Publishers, 2003), and Dr. Chalmers Johnson, *The Sorrows of Empire: Militarism, Secrecy, and the End of the Republic* (New York: Metropolitan Books, 2004).

4. A Chinese saying for something that seems as threatening as a tiger but is actually harmless or hollow. It was used frequently in relation to the U.S. invasion, occupation, and subsequent departure from Viet-Nam.

5. This quote came to me from a Colonel close to General Zinni, and was formally published in my article on "Open-Source Intelligence" in the six-volume set edited by Dr. Loch Johnson, *Strategic Intelligence* (Santa Barbara, CA: Praeger, 2006), Volume II, Chapter 6, pp. 95–122. The complete quote can be seen in a single "Graphic: Tony Zinni on 4% 'At Best,' at www.phibetaiota.net/2010/12 /graphic-tony-zinni-on-4-at-best/.

6. From direct unclassified conversation with two former Directors of the National Security Agency (NSA). I have also seen figures along these lines in writing over the years.

7. Two recent books capture the pathological inadequacies of the U.S. secret intelligence world and its denial of open sources of information: Dana Priest and William Arkin, *Top Secret America: The Rise of the New American Security State* (Boston: Little Brown, & Company, 2011); and Hamilton Bean, *No More Secrets: Open Source Information*

and the Reshaping of U.S. Intelligence (Santa Barbara, CA: Praeger, 2011).

8. Business Intelligence (BI) has changed to Competitive Intelligence (CI) and is now slowly evolving into Commercial Intelligence (CI). "Data-mining" is the correct synonym for what passes as BI today, being information delivered on a computer screen "dashboard" and drawing exclusively from internal sources. Now that the economic crash is wising up companies to the fact that the *last* thing they should be studying is their competitors, the new CI is focused on the five billion poor, what customers want, true-cost economics, and the arbitrage of opportunity rather than protection of market share in old markets.

9. Alvin Toffler, *War and Anti-War: Survival at the Dawn of the 21st Century* (Boston: Little, Brown & Company, 1993).

10. I remember learning this while working with the J-2 staff at U.S. Special Operations Command.

11. SECNAV INST 5000 allows government employees to do outside activities involving money provided their flag officer agrees, it does not interfere with their government job, and the lawyers concur. I tried to get the National Military Intelligence Association to do the conference, but they had a one-day conference with coffee mindset, and I knew we needed a three-day event with meals to bring in the internationals. I signed a contract for $25,000 with the McLean Hilton, not having the money, and managed to break even at $101,000, posting the detailed accounting on the first day; most attendees had no idea what it takes to create a new international event from scratch.

12. I went on to offer the conference for seventeen years, until it was stolen from me in 2007 and 2008 by a very unethical

person briefly employed by the U.S. government. The next "big thing" and the next big conference should be M4IS2.

13. Citation analysis was pioneered by Eugene Garfield, founder of the Institute for Scientific Information and its two main products, the Science Citation Index (SCI) and the Social Science Citation Index (SSCI). These track, both in online and reference book form, most academic citations. Knowing who has cited whom allows for analytics to show networks of information-sharing and influence, and to "map" the gaps between disciplines and sub-disciplines.

14. www.oss.net.

15. Personal communication from the chief of J-23 at U.S. SOCOM, whose single most brilliant contribution was to refuse to meet any requirement not entered into the all-source intelligence requirements database for the command. Within a year of starting operations, he was able to demonstrate this level of performance. No one else in the U.S. government, including the Open-Source Center at the CIA, has ever come close.

16. To understand the obstacles I faced, it is helpful to read my memorandum, "History of Opposition" (2004) at www. phibetaiota.net/2004/06/2004-modern-history-of-public -intelligence-and-the-opposition/ and see also the other thirteen items online at www.phibetaiota.net/category /archives/history-of-opposition/.

17. Other than my own work, the first book to look closely at the U.S. government application versus the needed democratic application of open-source intelligence is by Hamilton Bean, with a Foreword by Senator Gary Hart (D-CO), *No More Secrets: Open-Source Information and the Reshaping of U.S. Intelligence* (Santa Barbara, CA: Praeger, 2011).

18. Tom Atlee, *The Tao of Democracy: Using Co-Intelligence to Create a World That Works for All* (Charleston, SC: BookSurge Publishing, 2002). See also his newer book (which makes a fine follow-up to *The Open-Source Everything Manifesto*), *Empowering Public Wisdom: A Practical Vision of Citizen-Led Politics* (Berkeley, CA: Evolver Editions, 2012).

19. *Cf. Co-Evolution Quarterly* and *Whole Earth Review*, in their time the most *avant garde* of intellectual and cultural fermentation. See also Stewart Brand, *Whole Earth Discipline: An Ecopragmatist Manifesto* (New York: Viking Adult, 2009), and Howard Rheingold, *The Virtual Community: Homesteading on the Electronic Frontier* (Cambridge, MA: MIT Press, 2000).

20. Among the many books by Buckminster Fuller and Russell Ackoff, two stand out for me as most influential for this specific work: Buckminster Fuller, *Ideas and Integrities: A Spontaneous Autobiographical Disclosure* (New York: Macmillan Company, 1969), and Russell Ackoff, *Redesigning Society* (Stanford, CA: Stanford Business Books, 2003).

21. Pierre Teilhard de Chardin, *The Phenomenon of Man* (New York: Harper Perennial, 1976), and José Argüelles, *Manifesto for the Noosphere: The Next Stage in the Evolution of Human Consciousness* (Berkeley, CA: Evolver Editions, 2011).

22. See Riane Eisler, *The Chalice and the Blade: Our History, Our Future* (New York: HarperOne, 1988), and more recently, Carol Gilligan, Janie Ward, Jill McLean Taylor, and Betty Bardige (eds.), *Mapping the Moral Domain: A Contribution of Women's Thinking to Psychological Theory and Education* (Cambridge, MA: Harvard University Press, 1990).

23. *Cf.* Herbert Marcuse, *One-Dimensional Man: Studies in the Ideology of Advanced Industrial Society* (Boston: Beacon Press, 1991). Also *Eros and Civilization* (Florence, KY: Routledge,

1987) and *Counterrevolution and Revolt* (Boston: Beacon Press, 1989).

24. *Cf.* Tom Atlee, *The Tao of Democracy: Using Co-intelligence to Create a World That Works for All* (Charleston, SC: BookSurge Publishing, 2002); Barbara Marx Hubbard, *Conscious Evolution: Awakening Our Social Potential* (Novato, CA: New World Library, 1998); Juanita Brown and David Isaacs, *World Café: Shaping Our Futures Through Conversations That Matter* (San Francisco: Berrett-Koehler Publishers, 2005); and Harrison Owen, *Wave Rider: Leadership for High Performance in a Self-Organizing World* (San Francisco: Berrett-Koehler, 2008).

25. Online at http://ncdd.org/.

26. H.G. Wells, *World Brain* (Adamantine Press, 1993); Buckminster Fuller, *Ideas and Integrities: A Spontaneous Autobiographical Disclosure* (New York: Macmillan Company, 1969); Medard Gabel, *Designing a World that Works for All: How the Youth of the World are Creating Real-World Solutions for the UN Millennium Development Goals and Beyond* (Scotts Valley, CA: CreateSpace, 2010); Hans Swegen, *Global Mind* (London, UK: Minerva Press, 1995); Howard Bloom, *Global Brain: The Evolution of Mass Mind from the Big Bang to the 21st Century* (Hoboken, NJ: Wiley, 2001).

27. Alvin Toffler, *Revolutionary Wealth: How it will be created and how it will change our lives* (New York: Crown Business, 2007); Barry Carter, *Infinite Wealth: A New World of Collaboration and Abundance in the Knowledge Era* (Burlington, MA: Butterworth-Heinemann, 1999); Yochai Benkler *Wealth of Networks: How Social Production Transforms Markets and Freedom* (New Haven, CT: Yale University Press, 2007); Thomas Stewart, *Wealth of Knowledge: Intellectual Capital and the Twenty-First Century Organization* (New York: Crown Business: 2003).

28. Russell Ackoff, *Redesigning Society* (Stanford, CA: Stanford Business Books, 2003); John Warfield, *A Unified Systems Engineering Concept* (Columbus, OH: Battelle Memorial Institute, 1972); Kent Myers, *Reflexive Practice: Professional Thinking for a Turbulent World* (New York: Palgrave Macmillan, 2010).

29. Browse the categories by using the Books page or the bottom half of the middle column at www.phibetaiota.net.

30. Robert Fuller, *All Rise: Somebodies, Nobodies, and the Politics of Dignity* (San Francisco: Berrettt-Koehler Publishers, 2006); Dee Hock, *One from Many: VISA and the Rise of the Chaordic Organization* (San Francisco: Berrett-Koehler, 2005); C.K. Prahalad, *The Fortune at the Bottom of the Pyramid: Eradicating Poverty Through Profits* (Upper Saddle River, NJ: Pearson Prentice-Hall, 2009).

31. The first quotation is also the title, Shervin Pishevar, "Humans are the Routers," *TechCrunch*, 27 February 2011. The second is the very last sentence in James Bamford, *Body of Secrets: Anatomy of the Ultra-Secret National Security Agency* (New York: Anchor Books, 2002).

32. Herman Daly, *Ecological Economics: Principles and Applications* (Washington, DC: Island Press, 2010), and among others, *For the Common Good: Redirecting the Economy toward Community, the Environment, and a Sustainable Future* (Boston: Beacon Press, 1994); Paul Hawken, *The Ecology of Commerce: A Declaration of Sustainability* (New York: HarperBusiness, 2010), and with Amory Lovins and L. Hunter Lovins, *Natural Capitalism: Creating the Next Industrial Revolution* (New York: Back Bay Books, 2008); Charles Eisenstein, *Sacred Economics: Money, Gift, and Society in the Age of Transition* (Berkeley, CA: Evolver Editions, 2011).

33. I prefer DuckDuckGo to Wikipedia or Google for searches —here are the results for Richard Stallman online: http://duckduckgo.com/?q=Richard+Stallman.

34. The three best books on the hacker spirit remain Steven Levy, *Hackers: Heroes of the Computer Revolution* (O'Reilly Media, 2010); Sherry Turkle, *The Second Self: Computers and the Human Spirit* (Cambridge, MA: MIT Press, 2005); and Bruce Sterling, *The Hacker Crackdown: Law and Disorder on The Electronic Frontier* (New York: Bantam, 1993).

35. This was in 1994. Today the U.S. government is spending over $15 billion a year on the U.S. Cyber-Command, and in combination governments and corporations are spending billions on information security, something they will not achieve because our 1994 recommendations were ignored. Our letter can be viewed online at "1994 Sounding the Alarm," at www.phibetaiota.net/1994/08/1994-sounding -the-alarm-on-cyber-security/.

36. Free online at http://www.integrityatscaleblog.com/.

37. Michel Bauwens, "Occupy as a Culture Change Movement," P2P Foundation, re-posted to www.phibetaiota .net/2012/01/michel-bauwens-occupy-as-a-culture-change -movement/.

ROBERT DAVID STEELE (for Latinos, Robert David Steele Vivas) is a native of New York, born in 1952, who has lived all over the world, been a clandestine operations officer (spy) for the Central Intelligence Agency, and served as the second-ranking civilian in Marine Corps Intelligence. In the middle of a career as a secret intelligence professional he had a conversion experience. He realized that ninety percent of what was being done by way of very expensive secret intelligence was not useful to anyone, and that we were ignoring ninety percent of the relevant—usually open—information.

Educated at Muhlenberg College (Political Science), Lehigh University (International Relations), the University of Oklahoma (Public Administration), and the Naval War College (Defense Economics), he has spent most of his life in Latin America and Asia—including four years in Viet-Nam—as the son of an oil engineer. He also worked in Latin America as a clandestine case officer under cover,

THE OPEN-SOURCE EVERYTHING MANIFESTO

serving in El Salvador during a time of war, in Venezuela, and in Panama.

As a ghost-writer for the Commandant of the Marine Corps, then General Al Gray, he coined the phrase to explain why intelligence and communications must be managed together: "Communications without intelligence is noise; intelligence without communications is irrelevant." He went on to author many articles in the field of intelligence, for the *American Intelligence Journal* and the *International Journal of Intelligence and Counterintelligence,* and to write, edit, and publish eight books over a decade, ranging from *ON INTELLIGENCE: Spies and Secrecy in an Open World* (2000) to *INTELLIGENCE for EARTH: Clarity, Diversity, Integrity & Sustainability* (2010). His one political book, *ELECTION 2008: Lipstick on the Pig* (2008), contains chapters on The Substance of Governance, Legitimate Grievances, Candidates on the Issues, Balanced Budget 101, and a Call to Arms: Fund We Not Them.

As the #1 Amazon reviewer for non-fiction, reading in ninety-eight categories accessible via *Phi Beta Iota the Public Intelligence Blog* (www.phibetaiota.net), he has created a body of work featuring summary reviews of the public investigation and public intelligence produced by more than 1,700 other minds, which is now a free resource online.

Steele's "Open-Source Everything" philosophy—unusual for a former spy and senior civilian from the secret world—was presented in 2007 at Gnomedex, an annual gathering in Seattle of techno-bloggers. The keynote speech, "Open Everything: We Won, Let's Self-Govern,"

214

was videotaped and posted to the Web.[1] The full video as well as many remixes of portions of that presentation have become cult viewing within many communities, including Anonymous (the decentralized online community), LulzSec (a group of hacker activists in the public interest), and Occupy Wall Street ("Occupy" for short, the global rebellion against government and corporate corruption). Although this book was written prior to the emergence of the Occupy movement, it was adapted in early 2012 to better address the timeless reality of public protest in the face of great oppression.

In 2011 Robert Steele was accepted as one of two candidates for the Reform Party nomination for the presidential race in 2012, and put into one website for We the People Reform Coalition (http://bigbatusa.org) ideas developed by many non-partisan minds since 2000, including four fundamentals: Electoral Reform, Coalition Cabinet and Balanced Budget announced in advance of election day, and a commitment to True Cost Economics.

Robert is married and the father of three boys. The family is based in Oakton, Virginia.

Public Intelligence Blog: www.phibetaiota.net
We the People Reform Coalition: www.bigbatusa.org
About the Author: http://tinyurl.com/Steele2012

Author's Open Everything Keytone at Gnomedex 2007:
http://tinyurl.com/Open-Everything

EVOLVER EDITIONS promotes a new counterculture that recognizes humanity's visionary potential and takes tangible, pragmatic steps to realize it. EVOLVER EDITIONS explores the dynamics of personal, collective, and global change from a wide range of perspectives.

EVOLVER EDITIONS is an imprint of the nonprofit publishing house North Atlantic Books and is produced in collaboration with Evolver LLC, a company founded in 2007 that publishes the web magazine *Reality Sandwich* (www .realitysandwich.com), runs the social network Evolver.net (www.evolver.net), and recently launched a new series of live video seminars, Evolver Intensives (www.evolverinten -sives.com). Evolver also supports the Evolver Social Movement, which is building a global network of communities who collaborate, share knowledge, and engage in transformative practices.

For more information, please visit www.evolvereditions.com.